Get ready for
The Michigan ECPE C2
Speaking Test

For
English as Second Language (ESL)

Stavros Karathanasis
Ph.D., M.Sc.

First Edition 2020

Get ready for the Michigan ECPE C2 Speaking Test
For English as Second Language (ESL)
Certifications

Distributed By Amazon.com

ISBN: 978-618-84223-9-1 Paper Book

ISBN: 978-618-85040-0-4 (eBook, Kindle Edition)

The front cover photo is created by modifying free distributed photos by pixabay.com

Preface

This book has been designed to help candidates of the ECPE English language examination produce better results when dealing with the Speaking Part of the examination process. This Test requires the candidate to complete a verbal task at a proficient level of the English language. However, speaking English at this level is not something that comes naturally to people whose first language is not English. It requires systematic work and practice.

I don't claim to know everything about how to speak English fluently and sound like a native speaker. The knowledge contained in these pages has been developed and applied during my long-time study of English and is **based on a number of very good books and internet sites**. I hope this book will assist you in accomplishing your goals of passing the ECPE Speaking Test. However, despite the fact that the material contained in this book has been designed having in mind the ECPE Speaking Test, I hope it will be helpful to any candidate and regardless of the exam. It intends to take as many of the instructions given in this book essentially applicable to all test types.

As it has already been noticed, speaking is not theory. The good command of the language cannot be achieved only by reading a book. It requires practice, making mistakes and learning from them. It takes perseverance. But more than anything else, it is essential that you actually find someone who speaks English fluently and practice with them.

I wish you good luck and success in your Speaking Test.

Thessaloniki, Greece
September, 2020

Dr. Stavros Karathanasis

If you spot any error, please, let me know by sending me an email, at Karathanasis.Stav@gmail.com, so that to correct it when publishing the next version.

Introduction

It is expected that all candidates sitting for the ECPE be "proficient users" of the English language. This means that they should be able to complete a speaking activity by only collaborating with each other without getting support from the examiner. In other words, the candidates have to interact without getting help concerning language issues.

The candidate's linguistic ability (e.g. grammar, vocabulary, and pronunciation) is evaluated independently by two examiners and separately for each candidate. Apart from this, their ability to participate in an in-depth discussion with each other is also assessed. This means that no candidate should try to dominate during any stage of the test, neither play a passive role. On the contrary, both candidates are expected to contribute equally to the speaking activity.

Candidates are evaluated throughout every stage of the Speaking Test, which is designed that way so that each candidate is provided ample opportunity to speak individually and engage in discussions with their partner.

This book is divided in four (4) parts. Part I describes in full detail the Speaking Test and provides a variety of examples of how you can deal with any part of it and any difficulty you may encounter. Next, in Part II, a general example of a whole Speaking Test, as you will face in the examination time, a Speaking Model, is provided. Using this information, as well as the information given in Part I, you are asked to accomplish the practice tasks contained in Part III. After having dealt with these exercises, you will be able to cope with any particular Speaking Topic effectively. Finally, Part IV presents some examples of speaking tasks that you may come up against during the ECPE examination, along with three additional speaking tasks for further practice.

Dedicated
to my children

Katerina, Thalia, Polyxeni

Contents

Part II
A GENERAL MODEL OF THE SPEAKING TEST

Part III
DESCRIPTION OF THE SPEAKING TEST

PART IV
SPEAKING PROMPTS

Part I

DESCRIPTION OF THE SPEAKING TEST

1. Description of the Speaking Test

During the ECPE Speaking Test the candidates are required to interact both with each other and the examiner. There are two or maximum three candidates each time and two examiners. The examiners are present during the entire test; however only one of them interacts with the candidates each time.

The Test lasts from 25 to 35 minutes and consists of five stages (or parts) which are designed so that each candidate is provided with sufficient time to speak individually as well as to engage in a discussion with the other candidate and with the examiners. Stage I lasts approximately 3-5 minutes and Stage II through V last approximately 5-7 minutes each, while the tasks become more and more linguistically demanding from Stage I to Stage V.

In this Speaking Test, the full range of your speaking ability is assessed. You and the other candidate(s) should work together to complete an extended decision-making task.

The following short list presents the main steps of the Test:

Stage I: *Introduction (3-5 minutes)*

- The candidates introduce themselves in order to warm up and get to know each other, interact with each other and with the examiner and participate actively in the conversation.
- The first Examiner asks general questions.
- The examiner gives the candidates instructions how to process during each stage of the test.

Stage II: *Summarizing and recommending (5-7 minutes)*

- Each candidate is given an information sheet about a certain task with descriptions of two different options.
- The first candidate summarizes the points on his/her information sheet for both options.
- The second candidate recommends one of the options from the first

candidate's information sheet, briefly, giving reason(s) (not always necessary, though).
- Change of roles.
- The second candidate summarizes the points on his/her information sheet for both options.
- The first candidate recommends one of the options from the second candidate's information sheet, briefly, giving reasons (again, not always necessary).
- The candidates decide silently which of their own options they perceive as the best solution to the task.

Stage III: *Consensus reaching (5-7 minutes)*

- The candidates say which of their own options they have chosen.
- The candidates collaborate to narrow down their own two choices to one common choice, which represents the best course of action, by comparing and contrasting their chosen options and by discussing any advantages and disadvantages and, finally, agreeing on one option.

Stage IV: *Presenting and convincing (5-7 minutes)*
- The first Examiner introduces the second Examiner to the candidates.
- The candidates collaborate to decide on how to present and defend their common choice to the second Examiner making a plan of two short conversations.
- Each candidate makes a brief oral presentation to the examiner expressing two (2) reasons to justify why their final choice is the best so as to convince the second Examiner.

Stage V: *Justifying and defending (5-7 minutes)*
- The second Examiner asks each candidate challenging questions about their presentation in order to get them to defend their final choice
- The candidates justify their option giving reasons for the decision they have made in Stage III of the interview.

2. General Comments

There is no "wrong answer" in the Speaking Test, which means that you will not be graded on which option you choose. On the contrary, the examiners are more interested in the appropriateness and quality of the language you use as you work with your partner to make and justify your final decision.

In order to perform well in the Speaking Test you should focus on some features of the language. You have to demonstrate your ability of fluent speaking. To do so, use introductory and linking words and phrases as well as redundant language during your speech. Uncommon words and idioms will significantly improve your efficiency. Try to find words that are directly related to you topic. Whatever you are saying, say it with complex sentences using proper grammatical forms. Keep your tone quite formal and don't use slang or informal speech in your presentation. Become familiar with common expressions. Choose from these presented in this book, the ones that fit your personality most and practice them.

When you are describing your options to your partner paraphrase and restate the facts using your own words as much as possible and avoid reading from the task paper. On the other hand, when your partner is summarizing his/her options listen to his/her summary so that you can recommend one of his/her options. During the test you won't be allowed to look at your partner's info sheet until Stage IV. If you find it useful, you can take notes to remind you what was said.

3. Performing well throughout the Test

As all the warming-up questions will be open rather than closed ones you have to talk. Give as full an answer as you can so that you show the examiner you are acquainted with talking at length and able to communicate well. Use the transition signals to make your points stand out.

One problem with the Stages II – V of the ECPE Speaking Test is that candidates may end up saying the same things over and over again. A possible solution to this problem might be to elaborate. Invent some aspects of the subject and include them in your talking. It doesn't need to be real, unless they promote the discussion and are making your speech much easier. For example, if you are to propose a person for a grant, position etc., you are supposed to be acquaintances, you probably know more things about him/her than those stated in your information sheet.

This test is a short discussion about different options, so you have to speak for or against something intending to persuade your partner and the examiner. Do it by using appropriate expressions. When you present an argument (*arguing*), you should *always look at it from two sides, giving reasons why you agree or disagree before reaching a conclusion*. Sometimes it would be good to finish your answer with an example. In cases a *generalization* is required, avoid too many broad generalizations and use appropriate language (*Table 1*).

Paraphrasing is extremely important in oral examinations due to the fact that it can directly affect your performance raising your score. It means that you are saying or explaining something in your own words. In addition, you can and you should explain vocabulary gaps by paraphrasing the words you do not know in English. Paraphrasing is a verbal skill that can be developed. An effective way to use it in speaking tests is to pretend that you have forgotten a word, e.g. the word in question, let the examiner or the other candidate know that you have forgotten it, then you explain the word paraphrasing it, and finally you remember the word and you name it (related expressions are presented in *Table 2*). It really doesn't matter which word you paraphrase unless it is an uncommon one.

Apart from paraphrasing, you can use *placeholders* for unknown words. They are words that replace something you do not know or cannot remember its name. Such words are *thingummy, whatsitcalled, thingy, whatsit*. Even if you may think that the use of placeholders is not a very good way to impress the examiner keep in mind that this is exactly what native speakers do when they forget a word. So, when paraphrasing it would be good to use such words.

One further language feature that makes you sound like an English native speaker is **vague language**, *language that is not exact* (***Table 3***). A common example is the phrase *"or somewhat like that"*. Vague language is very common with numbers when expressing quantity, frequency or time. Lower numbers are often expressed by phrases such as *a couple of, a few*, whereas, larger numbers are rounded up with *about, around*, or replaced with *lots of, loads of*. With vague language, *"a couple"* does not usually mean *two*. It can mean *up to three* or even *four*. Do not use too many vague language words, e.g. list completers, in your speech. As a rule of thumb, three or four times in the whole process suffice.

Table 1. Common phrases used for making generalizations

• I'm inclined to be...	• In general,...
• I tend to be...	• In practise,...
• In most cases,...	• All things considered,...
• Generally speaking,...	• It is often claimed that...
• By and large,...	• Most people/experts believe that...
• On the whole,...	• To summarise,...
• Generally,...	• In conclusion I may say/I should say...

Table 2. Useful expressions that can be used in Paraphrasing

Begin paraphrasing	Explain a word
• I can't remember the English word; I will have to explain what I mean here,	• Well... is a kind /type of...
• Actually, I can't seem to remember the word; let me try to put it into plain words.	• It is actually something like...
• The word has slipped my mind; I will try to paraphrase it for you.	• In some ways it is similar to...
• I can't make out exactly what..., but it might be...	• And it is made from...
• I don't know the name of (this)... in English, but it's similar to...	• It is used by/for...
• I can't recall the exact word I'm looking for at the moment, but it means...	• it is often found in...
• I'm afraid I'm feeling a bit nervous and the word has slipped my mind.	• It involves...
	• One of the most unique features of X is that...

Remember the word
• Oh... I think I have just remembered it; the word I am looking for is X.

Table 3. Vague language	
Rounding up the time	**List completers**
• about half past eight • almost half past eight • it is/was half eight-ish • nearly half past eight	• ... and things like that (e.g. documentaries and things like that) • ... and stuff like that • ... and things (e.g. magazines and things) • ... and stuff • or something like that • or stuff like that • a/an... or whatever • to the... or whenever • with... or whoever
Playing with time	
• How can I put it? • Let me think... • That is a very interesting question. • This is a difficult question to answer. • I am glad you have asked that question.	
Round up numbers	**Finish answering questions**
• about 30 odd people • about 30 or so people • about 30-ish • a lot of/lots of/ loads of choices • a couple of times • a few times • about 10 or so • around 10 or so • just over sixty per cent • one in five/four... • 200,000 two hundred thousand (when the number is large don't add "s") • a large amount of • a little • a lot of • a small amount of • a small number of • few/fewer/ fewer and fewer • less/less and less • many/more/most/much • no/none of/ • several • the majority/minority of	• I think that is all I can tell you about... • I'm afraid that's all about... as much as I know. • I think that's about it. • I can't think of anything else right now. • Would you like me to tell you more about... ? • Is that all you'd like to know? • In conclusion, it seems that... • All things considered, it can be said that... • Taking everything into consideration, there is no doubt that... • Undoubtedly, we must say that,... • To sum up, it is obvious that... • All in all, it may be concluded that... • So, obviously...

There may be some times in the Speaking Test when you may not understand what the examiner or the other candidate is saying, or you did not hear something that was said due to the examiner's or the other candidate's strange accent or low voice, or because they may be speaking too softly or too quickly. At these times, do not be afraid to assert yourself or ask politely the examiner or your partner to speak more loudly, more slowly, to repeat his or her words (***ask for repetition***) or to clarify (***ask for clarification***) using other words.

If you have problems understanding a question, because the examiner is using words or phrases you do not know, or there is something you do not understand, ***ask for clarification***. If there is a word in the topic that you don't understand, don't hesitate to ask the examiner, or even your partner, to quickly explain that word to you, usually by paraphrasing it with an easier word or giving an example.

When you do this, you are showing the examiners that you have the skills needed to keep the conversation going. In the opposite case, the communication may break down; something undesired during the Speaking Test. Asking properly for clarification is part of any normal conversation, and shows your ability to react appropriately to this sort of situation. To act that way you can use phrases like these presented in ***Table 4b***.

If you are looking for ***clarification***, you could say what you think was asked or stated and then ask the interviewer or your partner to confirm it. Using questions, like these presented in ***Table 4***, the conversation will get back on track, and you will also have impressed the examiner with your conversation skills. Nevertheless, do not exaggerate. You cannot ask for clarification for everything. As a rule, if you ask for help or clarification two or three times, there will be no problem. However, if it happens more times then it may be a problem.

Apart from asking for clarification you may need to give clarification to your partner or even the examiner. In these cases, you can use expressions presented in ***Table 4d***. It is important to understand that by helping your partner and keeping the contributions to the conversation fairly equal you will be marked with more points. No one Speaking Test is a competition. You shouldn't ignore that and exclude your partner from the process otherwise you are likely to score less than in the case you involve your partner more in the conversation.

Table 4. The following sentence patterns may be of great help in the Speaking Test.

a. Stating the fact that you haven't understand something

	I didn't quite	catch that catch you get your point catch that catch the question follow what you were saying about "… " hear what you said	
Sorry, but I am sorry, but Excuse me, but I beg your pardon, but I'm afraid	I don't quite / really	know what you mean by "… " follow you understand understand you think I got your point understand / see what you are driving at / are getting at / are trying to say / mean by this / mean …	
	I'm not quite / exactly sure	clear about… clear about what you mean; with you I follow you I got your point I know what you mean I understand that I understand what you mean by… I understand what you mean	
	I missed	that one that the (first / last) part	
I can't even begin to understand what you are trying to say			

b. Asking for clarification

(but)	can could would	you (please)	ask it again be more specific clarify that elaborate on that explain that explain it explain what you mean by… give an example	(, please)?

Table 4. The following sentence patterns may be of great help in the Speaking Test.

put it differently
put it another way
repeat that
repeat it
repeat the question
run that by me one more time
say that again?

would you mind

asking it again?
being more specific?
clarifying that?
elaborating on that?
explaining that?
explaining it?
explaining what you mean by... ?   , please?
giving an example?
putting it differently?
puting it another way?
repeating that?
repeating it?
repeating the question?
saying that again?

could I ask you a little more about "... " in greater detail?
what do you mean?
what do you mean by saying... ?
I wonder if you could explain "... " in greater detail.
I wonder if you could say that in a different way.
This word is familiar to me, but I don't remember the meaning. Could you explain it?

Excuse me, could you speak up, please?
Would you please speak up? I cannot hear you clearly.
Would you please slow down until I get familiar with your accent?

c. Asking for confirmation

...

Are you trying to say that... ?
Did you say that... ?
Do you mean that... ?
If I understood correctly, you mean that...   Am I right?
Let me make sure I understand. Do you mean... ?   Is that right?
When you say... do you mean that... ?
You are saying... ?

Table 4. The following sentence patterns may be of great help in the Speaking Test.

d. Giving Clarification, Clearing up misunderstanding

what
all   I'm (was)   trying to say
                             saying

                                              is (was) that...

the point I'm (was) trying to make

            mean is...
What I meant was...
really meant by "... " is...
            meant to say was...
What I'm   saying is...
really   trying to say is...

                             another way
                             better
Sorry, let explain   it   further
me   put   that   in more detail
                             more clearly
                             differently

put   it
say   that   differently...

In other words...
That is to say...
That's not quite what I meant.
To be more specific,...
I'm afraid there seems to have been a slight misunderstanding.
Perhaps I should make myself clearer by saying...
By this I mean...
Let me explain/rephrase this

3.2. Interrupting politely

When you want to stop your partner or the examiner interrupting them, do not wait too long, you can *interrupt them politely*. You should do this by using appropriate expressions that show your speaking ability. *Table 5* presents some useful phases and sentence patterns you can use for this purpose.

Table 5. Phrases used to interrupt properly/politely

Coming back to a point	Interrupting
• As I was saying,...	• Before you go on,...
• As I have mentioned,...	• Before you move on...
• Coming back to...	• Anyhow,...
• To return to...	• By the way,...
• At the end of the day...	• Mmm. Good point. Anyway,...
• When all's said and done...	• Perhaps I could...
• If I could just finish what I'm saying...	• Can I just stop you there?
• Sorry, but could I just say something here...	• Excuse me for interrupting (you) but...
• To get back to the point at hand...	• Hold on a moment...
• To get back to what I was saying,...	• I am sorry to interrupt you...
• Can I bring you back to the previous point?	• Sorry to interrupt (you), but...
• I think I've already covered that	• I don't want to interrupt you, but...
• I'll be coming on that (point/ question) later.	• If I may just interrupt you for a moment, I would like to...
• If I can return to the original topic,...	• If I might interrupt for a moment,...
• I'm not sure that it is really very relevant	• Is this a good time to... ?
• Can I get back to you later on that?	• May/Can I interrupt (you) for a moment?
	• May I break in for a second?
	• This might be a good point to...
	• This might be the right time to say/ask...
Adding new information	
• Can I add here that... ?	• Another point I'd like to add about... is...
• Excuse me, but I would just like to point out that...	• Coming back to what was saying about... I'd also like to point out that...
• I'd just like to say that...	• I think it's important not to forget that...
• I'd like to add something here, if I may.	• The vast majority of people tend to think that...
• I'd like to comment on that...	• That reminds me of...
• I'd like to make a point...	• That is the next point I want to get to, once I've finished...
• It's also worth bearing in mind that...	

In the Speaking Test what is assessed by the examiners is your language ability, not your knowledge. So, do not hesitate to state that you cannot answer a question explaining why. You should do this by using appropriate expressions like the ones presented in *Table 6*, that show your speaking ability even if you don't possess the knowledge to answer the question rightly. Furthermore, in such cases, you can *hypothesize* the right answer or even *speculate* (*Table 7*). *Hypothesizing* means suggesting a possible explanation for something based on the information you have but without knowing whether the explanation is really true or not. *Speculating* means "*guessing*". Bear in mind, that in the test you may be deliberately asked to guess possible answers to a question about something.

Table 6. Phases expressing why you cannot answer a question

- Actually, to be frank, I really don't know very much about...
- I don't have much experience of... because... (but I guess...)
- I think if I had the opportunity to do something, I'd...
- I think it's still a bit soon for me to say, but I quite like the idea of...
- I think that... is something that...
- I'm afraid I cannot give you a satisfactory answer because... But I will try my best to...
- I'm not quite sure how to answer that question, but (perhaps)...
- Sorry, I have very little idea of... You see... (but I guess...)
- That's not an easy question to answer because...
- I can't say I'm terribly well-informed on the topic of... but I would imagine that the main arguments concern...
- It looks (to me) as if... but appearances can be misleading.
- That's a difficult question to answer because...
- That's a rather difficult question, but (maybe) I can answer you by saying...
- That's hard to say, but I would probably...
- There are several reasons I have this opinion, but I suppose it's mainly because...
- Well, it depends on whether or not I will...
- I'm afraid I'm not very knowledgeable on the topic of...
- Well, to tell you the truth, I've always liked...
- Actually, this is something that I have ever considered, but in short I suppose I would possibly... (consider doing this), especially if I had the chance to... (do this). If I... (did this) I would be able to... (do that) and I would also have the opportunity to... (do this).

If you hypothesize about something, you have to use conditional sentences in order to talk about something unreal and its consequences. When speculating about the future, an idea, a situation that is not certain, or about any unknown situation, you can use the future tense if you have a strong idea. When speculating on something of the past, you have to use the third-type unreal conditional sentences. When you want to talk about situations that were most likely untrue in the past you can use

- may have done
- might have done
- could have done

Must have done and ***can have done*** are used to make a guess that might likely happen in the past.

Hypothesize or speculate about something, answering a question of the type *"Do you think it will... ?"*, means that you are not sure about it. In these cases you can use hesitation expressions to state the **uncertainty** or **probability**. To express the level of certainty when discussing probability of some action that may or may not occur in the future, you can use one of the expressions suggested in ***Table 7***.

Table 7. Hypothesizing and Speculating

Hypothesizing		
Question	**Response**	
• Just imagine if you..., how would you..? • Suppose you did .., what would you do? • Just supposing you did..., what would it be like? • What if you were given a chance to do... ?	• Oh, if I had the chance, if I were...,	I suppose I'd... I might... I think I'd... I expect I'd... I would... I wouldn't...
	• I (don't) believe expect guess hope suppose think	I can... I will have to... I will... that... to have to...

Expressing probability	
• I bet it'll...	• No, definitely not.
• I don't think it'll...	• No, probably not.
• I doubt if it'll...	• Of course it won't...
• I expect it'll...	• Of course it'll...
• I suppose it might...	• Perhaps.
• I wouldn't be surprised if...	• There's a chance it'll...
• I'm absolutely sure it won't...	• There's no chance of...
• It might possibly...	• There's not much chance of...
• It's bound to...	• Yes, definitely.
• It's sure to...	• Yes, probably.

Table 7. Hypothesizing and Speculating

Speculating	
Question	**Response**
• What would you have done if... ? • What might have happened if... ? • How would you have felt if... ?	• Difficult to say, but I think I'd have... • I don't expect... • I don't think... would be more... than... • I expect to have to... first, as it is not very easy to... • I guess I will have to... • I hope I can... • I suppose I will have to... • I would guess that... is becoming more and more popular because... • I'd say it'll probably get better, because... • I'd say it'll probably get worse, because... • It probably won't... • It's hard to say but if I were to guess, I'd say that... because... • Oh, I don't know, I suppose I might have... • Well, of course, I could have...

Use hesitation devices expressing uncertainty	
• Actually,... • As a matter of fact,... • As far as I know... • As far I can remember... • How shall I put it? Let me put it in this way... • I am afraid I don't know it exactly, but... • I am not sure, but...	• In fact,... • It's like this, you see. • Let me see... • That's an interesting/a difficult question. I suppose/guess... • Well, I think/guess... • Well, it depends. • You see /know,...

Predicting	Expressing likelihood
• I would imagine that... would... • I would say that... would... • In all probability,... would... • It is possible that... might... • It is quite likely that... would... • Judging from...	• In all probability... • There is a good chance that... • It is quite probable that... It is quite likely that...

Table 7. Hypothesizing and Speculating

Expressing the level of probability	
Yes, definitely.	• Of course it'll... • It's sure/bound to...
Yes, probably.	• I expect it'll... • I wouldn't be surprised if it... + **V-ed** • I bet it'll...
Perhaps.	• There's a chance it'll... • It might possibly... • I suppose it might... •
No, probably not.	• I doubt if it'll... • I don't think it'll... • There's not much chance of it... + **V-ing**...
No, definitely not.	• Of course it won't... • There's no chance of it... + **V-ing**... • I'm absolutely sure it won't... • Apart from the fact that... I'm afraid I don't see an obvious connection between... • ... However, I have to admit that I can't... • I could hazard a guess that..., but I'm really not sure at all.

You should bear in mind that in this Speaking Test it's all about teamwork! You need to interact with the other candidate and not monopolize the conversation. So, when you finish speaking, you should say something that invites your partner to take part in the conversation or to find out what your partner thinks about (*Table 8*). This is particularly important when your partner seems hesitant to join in. Make a point by asking a leading question in order to help them start. This way you show the examiner that you know how to involve the other person in the conversation.

Furthermore, as the idea of the speaking task is to collaborate, not to dominate, your joint presentation has to sound like a team effort. For this reason you must use the pronoun **we** instead of **I** when presenting and justifying your ideas. Similarly, if you run out of things to say, don't hesitate to rely on your partner for help by asking them a question or inviting them to continue. The point is to keep the interaction moving.

Table 8. Phrases to be used for inviting your partner to participate

Signalizing the end of your presentation	Asking for opinion
• Well, that's my opinion and the reasons for it. • Well, that's all I wanted say.	• Do you agree or disagree? • Can I have your input on this? • How about... ? • How do you feel about this? • How do you feel about... ? • How does the idea of... appeal to you? • In my opinion..., would you go along with that? • What are you feelings regarding... ? • What are you views on/concerning... ? • What are your thoughts on this? • What do you think about/of... ? • What do you think about/of that? • What do you suggest? • What would you suggest? • What would you say about/ to... ? • What about... ? • What's your reaction/ response to this? • What's your point of view? • What's your take on this? • Where do you stand on this? • Would/Will it be a good idea if/to... ? • Wouldn't/Don't you agree that... ? • What's your opinion on the matter? • Do you agree with me that... ? • Do you think... would be of any use... ? • Well, it might... Do you agree that... would be useful in... ?
Asking for help	
• I'm not sure what else to say... • I have no idea where to begin. Any ideas?	
Providing help/Supporting	
• Did you notice... ? • In my experience,... What do you think,... (partner's name)? Have you observed that as well?	
Passing (Hanging) over the conversation to your partner	
• I think... (partner's name) point about the unpopularity of that option was a good one. • And now my partner would like to present more/his/her reasons for our choice. • And now, I'll let... (partner's name) share more reasons for choosing • Now, my partner would like to continue our presentation by telling you about...	

4. Performing well in each Stage of the Test

4.1. Stage I. Introduction/Breaking the Ice/ Small Talk

In Stage I the first Examiner and the candidates introduce themselves so that the candidates feel comfortable with each other. This is an ice-breaker/warm-up stage designed to get candidates to relax and get used to speaking with each other.

Firstly, the first Examiner is supposed to step out of the test room to greet you and invite you come in. After that, he/she introduces himself/herself and checks your identity, and asks you some simple questions such as greetings to help put you at ease. Similarly, when you enter the test room, you should greet the examiner. Apart from a moral obligation, this is really a great chance for you to make a first good impression showing your ability to communicate. *Table 9* lists some typical expressions of greeting and corresponding responds.

Table 9. Typical expressions of greeting and corresponding responds

Examiner's Greetings	Candidate's Greetings
• Good morning!	• Good morning!
• Good afternoon!	• Good afternoon!
• Good evening!	• Good evening!
• How are you today?	• Fine, thank you.
	• Fine, thanks.
• How do you do?	• How do you do?
• Hi, nice/good to meet you.	• Nice/Good to meet you, too.
	• I'm very glad to meet you.
	• It's my pleasure to meet you.
• Hi, how are you doing?	• Not too bad. And you?
• I haven't kept you waiting too long, have I?	• No. It doesn't matter.
• Come this way, please.	• Thank you.

After greetings, the examiner will begin by asking you some very general and easy questions about yourself (e.g. about your family, where you come from, your home town, your studies, your likes and dislikes, your hobbies, or what your interests are, etc.), the so called "getting-to-know-you" questions, which will help him/her find out a little about you. Then the examiner asks you (you and your partner) non-sensitive, factual background information (such as school/work/occupation, family/friends, hobbies/interests/leisure activities, plans for future vacation/travel, reasons for taking the Proficiency exam, and ambitions) (*Table 10*) or starts a conversation on one or more general topics related to the theme of the speaking task (*Table 11*). These questions are a warm-up to the rest of the test. The possible questions are innumerable. Those presented in these tables are only a small sample just to have an idea about them.

Although the first stage is a familiar conversation about the candidates' lives, it is demanded that candidates don't just sit passively waiting to be asked questions. You are expected to actively participate in the conversation by providing expanded responses and also by asking each other and the examiner questions that challenge/lead the examiner to ask for more information.

Table 10. Sample warm-up questions and possible answers that may be appeared in Stage I of the Speaking Test [Stage I: Introduction/Breaking the ice - Small Talk (3-5 minutes)].

Examiner's Questions	Candidate's Responses
• My name is... • My name is... and this is my colleague... • And your names are... ? • What's your name? • Could you tell me your full name, please?	• Sure. My name is Stavros Karathanasis
• Could I have your mark sheets, please? • And can I see your identification/ID card, please?	• Here you are.
• Thank you. • Thank you, that's fine.	• Please.

Table 10. Sample warm-up questions and possible answers that may be appeared in Stage I of the Speaking Test [Stage I: Introduction/Breaking the ice - Small Talk (3-5 minutes)].

Examiner's Questions	Candidate's Responses
• Now, first of all, in the first part of this interview/Test we'd like to know something about you by asking you some questions about yourself. • Could you tell me something about yourself/your family? • How old are you? • Are you married or single?	• I am 43 years old and I am married and have three children all of which are girls while two of them are identical twins. It is notably interesting to see them grow up and develop different characters. • *I'm... years old. I am a college/high school student. Or to be more precise, I'm on the... year of college/senior high school and my favorite subject at school is... Apart from this,... is my least favorite subject. In addition, I love traveling. So far, I've been to/visited... In the future I'd like to visit... as I have relatives/friends there.*
• *Do you have any brothers or sisters/ siblings?*	• *I'm the only child of the family.* • *There are three of us in my family and I'm the eldest/youngest of the three.* • *I come from a family of three/four children* • *I have a/two brother(s)/sister(s)/siblings.* • *My younger brother/elder sister goes to primary school and I go to junior/senior high school.*
• Can you tell me where you are from? • Where do you come from? • Where are you from? • Where did you grow up? • Where were you brought up? • Have you always lived there?	• Despite how easy it may be deemed, it is hard for me to say. To cut a long story short, I was born in Germany, but I moved almost immediately to my grandparent's village in Elassona, because my parents were running their own business in Germany and had

Examiner's Questions	Candidate's Responses
<ul><li>How long have you lived there?</li><li>Have you ever lived in any other place?</li><li>Where did you spend your childhood?</li></ul>	difficulty in taking care of me. After having spent my first four years of my life there, we moved to Trikala, a middle-sized city in Thessalia, which I consider as the place where I was grown up. At the age of 17 I left Trikala and came to Thessaloniki to study and since then I live here. I have been living here for 26 years. To conclude, I reckon that it is worth saying that, although I have spent the longest part of my life in Thessaloniki, I come from Trikala. <ul><li>*I come from/I'm from... (e.g. Trikala), a middle-sized city in... (e.g. Thessalia), but actually, I live about 30 kilometers out of the city - in a small town.*</li><li>*I live in... but I was born in...*</li><li>*I live on the eastern/western suburbs of the city.*</li></ul>
<ul><li>*What about your own childhood?*</li></ul>	<ul><li>*I've been living in... for... years.*</li><li>*I was born in this city, but we moved to... when I was... years old, because... So, I grew up in... Now, I consider... as my home town.*</li><li>*I was born in..., but I spent my childhood in another city, for I lived with my grandparents.*</li><li>*I live in... since I was born, and I never moved to other places. So, I spent my childhood in my home town.*</li><li>*I spent my childhood in my birthplace, but I went to another city to study/work.*</li><li>*I was born in... When I was... years old, my parents moved to... So, I was brought up there until I left for... to study at the age of...*</li></ul>

Table 10. Sample warm-up questions and possible answers that may be appeared in Stage I of the Speaking Test [Stage I: Introduction/Breaking the ice - Small Talk (3-5 minutes)].

Examiner's Questions	Candidate's Responses
	• *I lived there for 18 years. 10 years ago, I moved to... for my education.* • *I have been living there since I was born in 2002.*
• What kind of city is your home town? • Is it an attractive/pleasant place for visitors?	• Trikala is a middle-sized city which can get really crowded during the officials holidays so that you may think it is always a busy, bustling city. It is a lively city with lots of things to do and see, combining an old picturesque town with contemporary facilities like city-wide free internet access and electronically paid street parking. You can use your mobile phone to send a text message and pay for it. As Trikala is situated in a flat land it is suitable for cycling. This is the reason why there are so many bicycles in the city and most residents use them as a basic means of transport.
• Is it known for anything in particular? • Does your city have any historical importance? Are there any historic monuments there? • Are there any interesting places to see?	• The most fascinating points of the city are where the river Litheos flows through it, offering spectacular scenery, totally different from what may somebody be used to, especially at night when it is lightened up, and of course I should not forget the medieval castle. The castle, or more accurately the fortress, of the city, which was established in 400 a.D, provides a breathtaking view. Standing on the top of the hill overlooking the city, is awe-inspiring.
• What could a visitor see/do when they visit your home town? • What areas in your city or region	• If you are looking for a beautiful place to enjoy delicious food you shouldn't miss the opportunity to taste local grilled meet

Examiner's Questions	Candidate's Responses
would you recommend tourists visit and why? • What are the main tourist attractions in your home town? • If I visited your city, what would you advise me to go and see? • What can visitors do there? / What is there to see?	in Manavika, an old neighborhood which was used in the past to house greengrocers' storehouses. Now it has been turned into a restaurant district. The good thing about this place is that all buildings were restored taking into account the local architecture and their formal exterior design.
• Can you tell me more about your city/ town and what you like about it? • What part of the city do you live in?	• *It's a small/large village/town just outside/on the outskirts of...* • *... is a small town but it offers all the facilities a big city can offer.* • *It's a quiet/noisy/crowded/commercial/ industrial agricultural/suburban/residential area/neighborhood, very close to ... /the sea.* • *It's a neighborhood/an area where lots of students live.* • *It's on the outskirts of the city / in the city center / suburbs. It's the second / third largest city in this country.* • *It's a university town, so there are...*
• What kind of landscape surrounds your home town?	• *As... is located in... with a pleasant climate, the view there is wonderful. If you climb up the mountains, you can overlook the whole city enjoying the spectacular scenery. At night, the city is brightly lightened up by... The most interesting part here is the... and... Here we also have some unspoiled areas where you can experience..., and see a lot of natural habitats.*
• What is there for young people to do in... ?	• *There are a lot of things for young people to do. For example, they can go to sports clubs, internet cafes or to the cinema.*

Examiner's Questions	Candidate's Responses
	There are also clubs and cafes, fast food restaurants, bars and gyms.
	• *Visitors can see some archeological sites such as... and can go out and have fun as there are many bars, cafeterias and restaurants.*
	• *My home town is well known/famous for... throughout... (Greece, Europe)/all over the world.*
• Where do you live?	• I live in Pylea, a suburban town of Thessaloniki in a detached house which offers my family and me plenty of space, inside as well as outside the house, to spend our time and enjoy our lives. Furthermore, what I like more about it is that everything, my home, my job, and my children's school are conveniently located as they are only some minutes away from each other when using a car. For example, my job is only eleven (11) minutes from where I live and 6 minutes from my children's school. Checked many times and completely confirmed.
	• *At the moment I live in a small apartment/house which is not very far away from my university/school/job. But I would like to have a larger place to live in. Hopefully, one day I will.*
	• *I live in the downtown area, in a flat overlooking a busy road. It is a bit noisy, but very convenient.*
	• *I live on the suburbs/outskirts of the city, but I work in the downtown area, so I have to commute to and from work every day.*

Table 10. Sample warm-up questions and possible answers that may be appeared in Stage I of the Speaking Test [Stage I: Introduction/Breaking the ice - Small Talk (3-5 minutes)].

Examiner's Questions	Candidate's Responses
• *Are you working or studying at the moment?* • *Have you graduated or are you still studying?*	• *I'm still studying in... University, majoring in... (e.g. computing technology). I have one more year before I finish.* • *I'm now in the final year of my Master program, working on my dissertation. I enjoy my research a lot.* • *I graduated from University of Natural Sciences in... (e.g. 1994). My major was... (e.g. chemistry). By the time of my graduation, I was awarded the Bachelor of Science in the field of chemistry.* • *I took the entrance examination into... University, majoring in engineering. I studied... for 4 years and graduated in... After that, I went on with a postgraduate course in another university for two years.* • *I went to... University of... to study... for... years and got a Bachelor's degree.* • *I work/am employed part-time/ full-time, doing...* • *I attend private/state school* • *I am presently in junior/senior high school* • *I am attending the 3rd grade of senior high school* • *I am in University...* • *I attend University...*
• Can/Could you tell me something about your education/educational background? • What was/is your major?	• I studied physics at Aristotle's University of Thessaloniki and graduated from the Faculty of Science, School of Physics, almost 22 years ago. Afterwards I went on with postgraduate courses in the same University for two years and got a Master of Science in Environmental Physics. Next, I integrated my academic education

Table 10. Sample warm-up questions and possible answers that may be appeared in Stage I of the Speaking Test [Stage I: Introduction/Breaking the ice - Small Talk (3-5 minutes)].

Examiner's Questions	Candidate's Responses
	in 2002 by being awarded the PhD in Physics. In the meanwhile, I was applied to work for the public sector as an environmental physicist a position that I hold until now. I have been working there for 15 years and I am being regarded as an expert in environmental issues.
• What did you major in? • Why did you choose physics as your major? • How do you like your major?	• I have chosen my major just because I love it and studying it gave me a lot of satisfaction. To be a physicist is what I have always dreamed of since I was a child. I was always fond of discovering how nature works.
• What do you do for a living?	• I work in the public sector in the Directorate General for Spatial and Environmental Policy of the Decentralized Administration of Macedonia and Thrace as an environmental physicist.

	• *I'm working as a/an...*
	  o *secretary to the manager*
	  o *systems analyst in a computer company*
	  o *tour guide*
	  o *computer programmer*
	• *I'm in charge of... (e.g. office management), ... (e.g. doing some complicated personal relationship)*
	• *I'm working for a... company as a/an..., specializing in...*
	• *I worked as a/an... in a/an... company, but changed my career in... (2010).*
	• *I have been working for...*

Table 10. Sample warm-up questions and possible answers that may be appeared in Stage I of the Speaking Test [Stage I: Introduction/Breaking the ice - Small Talk (3-5 minutes)].

Examiner's Questions	Candidate's Responses
	• *I can't find work in my field of expertise as the job market is saturated.* • *It is tough enough to find a job...*
• *What do your parents do for a living?*	• *My father is a /doctor/lawyer/civil engineer and my mother is a civil servant/shop assistant*
• What does your work involve? • What are some of your responsibilities/ your work routine?	• My work involves dealing with environmental issues and in particular those ones related to the Environmental Permitting. Examining of Environmental Impact Statements and approval of them are the main responsibilities it entails. To elaborate it, I have been working on the mitigation of the environmental impacts that may have a vast variety of activities and projects such as industrial plants, renewable power sources, such as wind farms, photovoltaic, biomass and biogas production and use in power production, telecommunication antennas and radio and television broadcasting installations. I have to admit that I learnt many things and acquired essential knowledge all these years I have dealt with such issues. And, of course, this is because I work hard to keep myself informed about the latest developments in this field, especially environmental European and National legislation.
	• As a final point, if time permits, I would roughly describe you the procedure resulting in an Environmental permit as I think it is interesting and worth being known by everyone.

Table 10. Sample warm-up questions and possible answers that may be appeared in Stage I of the Speaking Test [Stage I: Introduction/Breaking the ice - Small Talk (3-5 minutes)].

Examiner's Questions	Candidate's Responses

	• To begin with, the interested part, either an individual or a company, has to hire a researcher or a researching group to carry out the necessary investigation and survey procedures leading to a document, the Environmental Impact Statement. This assesses the potential impacts their intended activity or project may have to the environment. This document should also describe the required measures they will take in order to eliminate or mitigate these impacts. I check the document and, after consulting other responsible authorities, I propose a number of environmental conditions, limitations and restrictions to be complied with by the constructor of the project as well as its owner, the entrepreneur, in order to make it environmentally friendly.
	
	• *I'm a/an... and I have to..., and...*
	• *I often have to...*
	• *My work involves...*
	  o *making computer programs for my colleagues*
	  o *doing market research*
	  o *typing some business letters*
	  o *arranging meetings, interviews, appointments and schedules for the manager*
	  o *working on projects*
	  o *making specialized programs for... (e.g. educational) purpose*
	  o *advising my clients on how to improve their productivity*
	  o *meeting with clients*
	  o *sending the feedback from the staff and clients.*

Table 10. Sample warm-up questions and possible answers that may be appeared in Stage I of the Speaking Test [Stage I: Introduction/Breaking the ice - Small Talk (3-5 minutes)].

Examiner's Questions	Candidate's Responses
	o *checking e-mails or instructions from my boss* o *studying data and make analysis* o *giving instructions to the... about the...* o *surfing the Internet to get some information about the latest development in the field*
• What would your dream job be? • Which careers really interest you?	• To be a researcher in Physics and indeed a university professor was my ideal career, as I wanted to work with something challenging while discovering new things. However, having a family was, and still remains so, more important to me than to pursue an academic career. Furthermore, given the high unemployment's rates and the demanding conditions associated with such a profession and especially the waiting period until being elected (*or selected*) I do not regret not finally following this career.
• What do you like/enjoy about your job?	• To be frank, working in the public sector cannot be seen as a challenging job as anyone would like, but I like my job. Let me explain it further. The pay is pretty good, much better than it would be if I worked for a moderate company or was a freelance, which is the rule. In addition, the work conditions and the work environment are incomparable, my colleagues are very kind to me and we get on well with each other. Last but not least, the job isn't so difficult.

Examiner's Questions	Candidate's Responses
• What gives you job satisfaction?	• It is not only the financial reward but the psychological well-being that really counts. It is the self-fulfillment that brings me pleasure. The dealing with taxing environmental issues and tackling the problems they entail gives me a sense of accomplishment. Moreover, I get on well with all my colleagues providing me a pleasant environment to pass a large part of my day.
• How much free time do you have at the moment? • How do you spend your free/ spare time? • What do you like to do in your free time? • How do you usually spend your free time?	• Well, as far as free time is concerned, I haven't got much, to be honest, as my family uses it up. However, whenever I do find some I prefer to read a book or something on the internet, especially before bedtime. Sometimes, when free time suffices I enjoy going for long walks either alone or with a friend of mine or just hanging about around the town or going out with friends for a coffee. In the summer, I enjoy going for long walks by the sea or hiking.
• What kinds of hobbies or leisure time activities are you interested in?	• Well, as far as free time is concerned, I haven't got much, to be honest, as my family uses it up. However, I am interested in something I consider quite unusual. The last three years I have been getting involved in the study and construction of a solar oven. How to use solar energy to cook your meal. Such type of activities have always attracted me since I was a child. So, it is not surprising why my fellow student and my friend used to call me "Inventor".

Examiner's Questions	Candidate's Responses
	• To elaborate it, a solar oven is a simple device that uses mirrors to redirect solar beams, and hence the solar heat, into an appropriate cooking vessel, usually a thin black pot covered with a glass lid. Its design and the material used to construct it contribute significantly to its efficiency. So far, I have constructed some prototypes and cooked lentil soup and pasta. However, I need a little more time to study them and conduct further experiments and I hope that my English command will help me as the needed information about this topic is published in English.
	• *I've got a really tight schedule with my schoolwork but when I do find some free time, I love surfing the net or going out with friends for a coffee. In the summer, I enjoy going for long walks by the sea, jogging, playing sports, hanging out in the town and hiking in the hills.*
	• *I don't have much free time... because I have private French lessons on Mondays, Wednesdays, and Fridays.*
	• *I swim/run to keep fit because keeping fit is important.*
• Do you have any ambitions? • What are your ambitions? • How easy or hard will it be to achieve those ambitions? • Apart from work, what other ambitions do you have? • What's your biggest ambition in life? • What are your plans for the future?	• To be honest, I haven't given it much thought yet, but I suppose my dream would be to live a full and happy life. In addition, I would like to continue communicating openly with my children and give them more compliments and praise. In order children to be able to develop imagination, creativity, perseverance and independence we ought to spend as much as possible time we

Table 10. Sample warm-up questions and possible answers that may be appeared in Stage I of the Speaking Test [Stage I: Introduction/Breaking the ice - Small Talk (3-5 minutes)].

Examiner's Questions	Candidate's Responses
	can, with them. However, nowadays there is lack of communication and children often feel neglected, instead. • *I want to get a degree in...* • *I want to study abroad...* • *I will be taking university entrance exams to...* • *I want to study/set trained to be/get trained...* • *I graduate this year, so...* • *I want to study languages...*
• *What would you like to be doing in ten years' time?* • *Where do you see yourself in ten years' time?*	• *I am hoping to study/work as... because...* • *I have always been interested in... so...* • *First and foremost, I hope I graduate from high school with a decent grade, and get into University. I would really like to become a/an...* • *In ten years' time I imagine I will have finished my studies. Apart from that, I would welcome the opportunity to travel, as I am fond of meeting new people and visiting other countries. Additionally, I would like to have found a satisfactory job, making me feel content, and being relevant to my qualities and qualifications. I think that my goals are not extremely easy to achieve as they require a lot of studying and patience.*
• Why are you learning English? • Why is English important to your future?	• It's an advantage to have the Certificate of Proficiency in English on your resume. It's recognized by both the private and the public sector. English has become the global common language of our times and I believe that anyone who wants to pursue a career should be able to speak

Table 10. Sample warm-up questions and possible answers that may be appeared in Stage I of the Speaking Test [Stage I: Introduction/Breaking the ice - Small Talk (3-5 minutes)].

Examiner's Questions	Candidate's Responses
	and write it on an advanced level. By mastering English not only can we broaden our horizons but also obtain valuable knowledge as the vast majority of it is published in English. Apart from that, English can affect considerably the way we think as we can be acquainted with many new ideas coming up in every part of the world. Furthermore, being fluent in English will make me able to communicate easily with scientists of other countries who are interested in the same scientific field. To sum up, English is a very important qualification and it certainly provides individuals with valuable knowledge.
• What made you choose a Proficiency course? • What do you need the certificate of Proficiency for? • How useful will it be in the future?	• I have been learning English by self-study and that is why it took me so long to master it. After a lot of effort I realized that the only way to master it is to set a specific and measureable goal: to get a renowned certificate in English and I opt for ECPE.
• *What do you need the certificate of Proficiency for?*	• *I chose Proficiency in order to master English as it is a requirement for college admission.* • *The certificate of proficiency in English will help me find a job more easily.*
• How long have you been studying English?	• I have being learning English longer than you can imagine. To begin with, I've been studying English for about 22 years. I learned English by self-study and that is why it took me so long to master it. The first time I seriously came up against the

Table 10. Sample warm-up questions and possible answers that may be appeared in Stage I of the Speaking Test [Stage I: Introduction/Breaking the ice - Small Talk (3-5 minutes)].

Examiner's Questions	Candidate's Responses
	need to deal with something written in English was when I had entered my postgraduate Courses. A professor assigned me a project and I asked him for bibliography in German. He opened his eyes wide and told me that as long as I wanted to accomplish that task I had at least to be able to read English papers. After that I was trying to learn English on my own for many years. Only recently did I realize that the only way to achieve this is to set a specific and measureable goal: to get a renowned certificate in English and I opt for ECPE.
• Do you have any pets? • If not, would you like to have any? Why? Why not?	• I think a pet can bring happiness and be a companion to play with but it is also a great responsibility. Nevertheless, my three children occupy the largest part of my time and do not leave any space for a pet.
• In order to be able to navigate the conversation in your advantage, (namely to patronize the discussion) you can use some of these phrases and/or sentences	• To say only a few things. However, I reckon I could add some particularly interesting information if you like. • That's all for the moment, as I think I have to be brief. Otherwise, I think I could reveal you a couple of notable and worthwhile elements about... • To give you only a brief but concise answer, I hope. However, if this has triggered your curiosity I can satisfy it by unveiling some more details.

Issue	Possible questions about it
Exercise and sports	• Are you able to make time in your schedule to play sports or get regular exercise?
Education	• What plans do you have after you graduate your current school? • Where would you like to study; at a university where you could live at home or at a university where you would live in a dormitory or apartment and come home only infrequently?
Health care	• If you could make one change in the health care system of your country, what would it be?
Leisure time	• What do you do in your spare time? • What are your hobbies?
Pets	• Have you ever had a pet? If so, who took care of the pet? Was it you or someone else in your family? If not could you explain why not? Do you see yourself owning a pet in the future? • What are some of the advantages or disadvantages of pet ownership for families with children?
Cultural heritage	• What museums does your hometown have?
Environment	• Do you think people are overly concerned about protecting the environment these days or do you think there is real cause for people to be worried? • In terms of local problems, what do you think people in your area are most concerned about? And why? • What role could an individual play in terms of doing something to protect the environment?
Other issues	• Have you ever attended a summer course? • What kind of holidays do you prefer? • Would you like to live in a big city or in the countryside?

All the questions will be **open questions** rather than **closed questions**. A *closed question* is one that can be answered by a single word (by Yes or No) or a couple of words. In fact, you will not get a question that could be just answered by Yes or No. Such questions may begin like this

- Have you...,
- Have you got any...,
- Do you...,
- Is it... etc.

On the other hand, an *open question* asks the candidate to give an extended answer. These questions have the form:

- Can you tell me about... ?

In these cases, by answering the question you also have to explain why and this is a golden opportunity for you to show how good your English is. The goal is to let the examiner hear plenty of English which will help him or her evaluate you. So, make good use of this opportunity and give an extended answer, giving more information by describing, explaining, and offering examples that help you support a statement. However, do not just ramble on in order to keep talking. Give reasonably short answers, just enough to answer the question. You need to be coherent and able to take turns.

As in any Speaking Test or Oral Examination, there are some common types of questions that are almost always emerged. They are introduced using the wording:

- When... ?
- What... ? What... is? To what extent do you think... ?
- Where... ?
- How... ? How often you do this? How do you feel about... ? How far do you think... ?
- Why... ? Why you like it? Why do you think that... ?
- Whether it is... or not.
- Do you think... ?
- Is... important, do you think?

All these questions can be answered in a similar way: using appropriate structures that contain linking words and phrases combining complex sentences. It would be preferable not to repeat the topic word in the detail sentences. Instead, you could use *"it"* or *"they"*. In addition, in the detail sentence it would be good if you use a linking word such as *"in fact"*. Examples that can be used in these structures are presented in *Table 12.* A typical overall answer may look like this:

Lead-in phrase +
Introductory/opening phrase +
topic/1st point +
linking word/phrase +
details about the topic/1st point +
connective phrase +
2nd point +...
and so on.

Don't waste time by learning and memorizing every possible linking phrase or structure. Chose one or two and practice them in order to became perfect and seem natural.

In any case, a good response has the following traits:

- It is long enough but doesn't move away from the topic.
- It contains
    - redundant language
    - linking words and phrases
    - one idiom
    - complex structures
    - a mix of tenses
    - some uncommon vocabulary
- The vocabulary is topic-specific
- The grammar is correct

Table 12. Phrases that can be used to describe things, thoughts, persons, etc.

Lead-in phrases that buy time

- Actually,...
- Actually, to be fair...
- Alright then,...
- Alright,...
- As a matter of fact,...
- Certainly...
- In actual fact...
- In fact, in all honesty...
- In fact,...
- Initially then,...
- Of course...
- Of course you know...
- Of course, it goes without saying...
- OK in general...
- OK then,...
- OK, certainly...
- Frankly,...
- To be (quite) honest/frank,...
- I wonder...
- The thing is...
- It's like this, you see...
- What I'm trying to say is...
- What I would say is...
- Let's put it this way...
- I'll tell you what...
- OK, well in reality,...
- Right, OK...
- So I suppose I...
- So, to start with,...
- Sure, obviously...
- Well,...
- Well, actually...
- Well, certainly in some way...
- Well, first of all...
- Well, in actual fact,...
- Well, in all fairness...
- Well, in truth...
- Well, quite honestly...
- Well, to be honest...
- Well, you know...
- Well...
- Um... / er...
- You know/ see...
- I see.
- I mean...
- Let's see (now).
- Now let me think/see.
- I'll have to think about it.

opening, introductory or getting started phrase

- ... I guess I could start off by saying that...
- ... I could get started by stating that...
- ... I should commence by saying that...
- ... I could start off by saying that...
- ... I need to start off by pointing out that...
- ... I suppose I should begin by highlighting the fact that...
- ... in reply to the question...
- ... in response to the question...

• ... I would like to begin	• by pointing out that... • by raising the issue of... • by saying that... • with...
• ... I would like to	• comment on the problem of... • get started by looking at...

expanding a point	linking word for expansion
• … and what I would like to add here is that…	• because/due to/owning to/as/since
• … and what I need to emphasize here is that…	• for the reason that
• … and what I ought to stress here is that…	• Therefore
• … and what I have to mention here is that…	• as a result (of which)
• … and the thing that needs to be highlighted here is that…	• for the above mentioned reasons
• I would like to explain that…	• in fact
• You really have to understand that…	• at which point
• I suppose I should underline the fact that…	• although
• What I would like to make clear is that…	• consequently
• What I would like to shed light on here is that…	• particularly
	• in particular
	• especially

introducing the first point phrase

- … the first thing I should mention is that…
- … the first point I would like to make is…
- … there are several points I would like to make…
- … there is a number of points I would like to make…
- … there is a mixed variety of…
- … there is quite a wide range of…
- … there is a fairly broad range of…
- … there is an extensive diversity of…
- … there is quite a diverse mixture of…
- … the point I would like to begin with is that…
- … the main thing you need to know is that…
- … you may be aware that in fact…
- … you may not be aware that in fact…
- But I guess the most + **adjective** + **topic** would probably be…
- However, I suppose the most + **adjective** + **topic** could possibly be…
- Though I think the most + **adjective** + **topic** would potentially be…
- Yet I imagine the most + **adjective** + **topic** may well be…
- Still, I suppose that the most + **adjective** + **topic** could perhaps be…

introducing the third point

- Proceeding with the issue of…
- Moving forward onto the area of…
- And I shouldn't forget to mention that…
- In addition to what I have just said, I can add that…
- Something else that I need to comment on is that…
- I guess I could also remark on the fact that…

introducing the fourth (last) point

- Finally then, if there is time,...
- To end with, if I still have time, I could add...
- As a final point, if time permits, I would like to bring the point of...
- To cut a long story short, as my very last point, with reference to my options of...
- On final point which may have escaped your notice concern...

introducing the second point

- Going on the next point which I would like to make is...
- Continuing then with the next point of...
- Next then in response to the point of...
- One further point I would like to bring to your attention is...
- Another point which I could add is that...
- A second feature which I should mention is that...
- As well as that, I could say that...
- On the top of that I can also add that...
- Also, I suppose I should say that...

adjectives

advisable	famous	notorious	trendy
common	fashionable	popular	up-to-date
commonly-used	frequent	preferable	usual
commonplace	important	prominent	well-known
crucial	influential	renowned	widely-known
current	normal	significant	widely-used
customary (normal)	notable	standard	widespread

Adding detail

- The thing with... is that... In fact,...
- I assume... are so + **adjective**, because... In fact,...
- The point I want to add about... is that... In fact,...
- And what you have to know about... is that... In fact,...
- And what you have to realize with... is that... In fact,...
- And the explanation for this could be that... In fact,...
- And the basis for this is that... In fact,...
- And the main characteristic of... is...
- And the unique aspect of... is...
- And one exceptional aspect with... is that...

Table 12. Phrases that can be used to describe things, thoughts, persons, etc.	
Adding a second type	
• Besides...,... • As well as...,... / In addition to...,... • ... another kind of... would be... • ... another form of... worth mentioning could be... • ... a second variety of... would be something like... • ... a subsequent category would be something like...	
Last point	
• ... although these are not as + **adjective** + as the first (two) that I mentioned	
Vague language	
• And of course there is the usual things like... and...	• Likewise, as might be expected, there are things like... and...
• And obviously you can also find things like... and...	• And naturally, there are things like... and...

Expressing likes and dislikes is an important area of English language. Thus why there is a wide range of related expressions of appropriate language that you are supposed to be able to use them. When you are asked if or whether you like something ("*do you like... ?*") avoid using simple vocabulary (such as like, dislike, enjoy, love, hate). Instead, use alternative more sophisticated expressions that display your ability to express yourself skillfully. Simple expressions may be used by the examiners in their question and you should not recycle these words in the form of a statement.

In general, if you are asked by the examiner whether you like something, give a positive (yes) answer even if it is not true. Similarly, if you are asked if there is anything you don't like give again a positive answer. This is preferable as it is much easier to speak positively, explaining *why you do something*, than negatively, explaining *why you do not do something*. Lastly, putting "*like expressions*" and "*dislike expressions*" in the same answer is not wrong. However, such answers are quite long, so it is better to split them into two separate parts. When expressing likes and dislikes try to use three or four liking or disliking expressions in your answer (***Table 13***).

opening phrases

- I would say that...
- I suppose that for the most part I would probably say that...
- I should really say that...
- I think I would have to say that...
- I would definitely say that...
- I guess that generally speaking I would certainly say that...

expressing like

- I am fairly/pretty keen on...   *(be keen on something or someone = be enthusiastic about something or someone)*
- I am quite/pretty fond of...   *(fond of somebody = feeling affection for someone, especially someone you have known for a long time fond of (doing) something = finding something pleasant or enjoyable, especially something you have liked or enjoyed for a long time)*
- I'm into...
- I am really into...
- I like nothing more than...
- I am quite a big fan of...
- I simply adore...
- I am quite enthusiastic about...
- I generally prefer... (use only when comparing)
- I am totally mad about...
- I am quite passionate about...
- I am quite partial to...   *(be/get partial to something or someone = favoring or preferring someone or something)*
- I really like the way...
- I am not ken on...
- I am a keen/avid (surfer)
- I am keen on/fond of (surfing)
- I like nothing more than (going surfing)
- I am itching to try/go... (I really want to)

expressing dislike

- I am not ken on...
- I am not so keen on...
- I am not much of a fan of...
- I am not really that fond of...

expressing strong dislike

- I totally detest...
- I absolutely loath...
- I really can't stand...

Table 13. Phrases that can be used to express likes and dislikes	
introducing reason	**introducing detail**
• And I guess this is probably because...	• ... but in particular...
• This could be because...	• ... particularly...
• This might be because...	• ... especially...
• This could be due to the fact that...	• ... specifically...
• This might be due to the fact that...	• ... to be more precise...
• This is due to the fact that...	• ... to be more specific...
• I suppose the reason has something to do with the fact that...	• ... to be more exact...
	• ... to be more accurate...
adding a second point	
• As well as this...	• Additionally,...
• In addition to this...	• Furthermore,...
• To add to this...	• Beside,...
• In addition,...	• I might add that...
Balancing	
• On the other hand...	• Apart from...
• Although..., we mustn't forget...	• However,...
• Despite/In spite of the fact that that..., I still think...	• Still,...

When you are asked questions about *How often you do something or Where you usually do something or When you do something or At what time of the day you usually do something or Who you spend your free time with* you are not obliged to give a direct answer. In the contrary, the best and easier way to answer is also the most beneficial: provide an answer of the kind *"it depends"*, choosing to contrast two related situations that are very different (warmth/cold, light/dark, summer/winter) including *"if"* and *"will"* in your response for each situation.

So, in order to answer in the most impressive way you should select a **lead-in phrase**, then a ***"depends" structure*** using a linking phrase to introduce the ***first situation*** with a conditional structure. Next **compare** the first with the second situation, using ***comparing or contrasting linking words or phrases*** (***Table 14***).

There are questions (e.g. *Are you good at doing this? Do you think doing this is better than doing that? Will you do this if you do that? Have you been doing this long? Are there any interesting places to visit in... place? Did you like this?*) that could be answered with a direct yes or not. It is not wrong to answer that way, but these responses are often too simple and do not display any particular ability in speaking. It is preferable to give a both yes and no answer.

Table 14. Phrases that can be used to say how, how often or when you do something

"depends" phrases
• ... I think I would have to say that it really depends on...
• ... I suppose I would have to maintain that it depends really on...
• ... I imagine that it would depend on the situation.
• ... I guess my answer would be determined by different conditions.

expanding	comparing or contrasting
• For example...	• Whereas in contrast...
• More specific...	• While on the other hand...
• To be more exact,...	• Though, at the same time...
• More precisely like...	• While, oppositely...
• To be more direct,...	

Conditional structures	
If... (1st/2nd situation) then	• I will most likely do this
	• it is quite possible that I will do this
	• as a consequence I will probably do this
	• I guess it is quite possible that I will do this
	• it is more likely that I will do this
	• it is almost certain that I will do this
	• I will almost always do this
	• I will most certainly do this

As it is already been presented in the previous paragraphs, begin your answer using a *lead-in phrase*, then make your *affirmative statement* (*yes answer*) and next develop it using a *linking phrase* (*Table 15*). After that, introduce the *negative statement* (*no answer*) with an appropriate *linking phrase* and develop it like you did with the yes answer. Finally, round–off the whole answer. Nevertheless, keep in mind that in some questions it may be difficult to answer both yes and no. In these cases it would be probably much easier to provide a positive answer using the above displayed structure and then expand it with a couple of reasons.

Questions of this type *Would you like to do this? Would you like to be this? What do you do if you have this? What will you do if this is like that then? What would you do if you did this? What would you have done if you hadn't done this?* require an answer that contains a second conditional structure (*if + I + past simple, I +would/ could/ might + bare infinitive*) in order to talk about either a present or future time describing an event that is unlikely (hypothetical).

Table 15. Phrases that can be used to answer Yes and No questions

Alternative way to say Yes		Alternative way to say No	
• certainly	• I'm afraid not	• no way	• of course not
• certainly not	• I'm afraid so	• not at all	• without a doubt
• definitely	• indeed	• not really	• you must be kidding
• for sure	• naturally	• of course	
introducing the first part			
• ... if I think about it, I guess in many ways...			
• ... I suppose that to some extent...			
• ... I guess that on the one hand...			
linking structure			
• ... especially when you consider that...			
• ... particularly if you think about the point that...			
• ... especially with regard to the point that...			
• ... and this is definitely the case with...			
introducing the second part			
• But you also have to understand that...			
• Even so, you could also say that...			
• At the same time, you could say that...			
rounding–off answers			
• So, all in all, I guess my answer would have to be yes and no			
• So, on the whole, I suppose the answer has to be yes and no			
• So, all things considered I guess the answer is both yes and no			
• So, in the main, I suppose the answer is probably yes and no			

Begin your answer using an introductory phrase, then formulate a second conditional structure and after that add a reason or some detail discussing the benefits or the drawbacks if your answer has a negative aspect (***Table 16***). Moreover, in some cases, you may need to use more second conditional structures. ***Table 17*** summarizes the possible question types presented in the previous paragraphs and suggested general answers.

Table 16. Phrases that can be used to answer hypothetical questions		
introductory phrase		
• I do not think I have ever thought about that, but		• I guess... • I imagine...
• This is not something that I have ever considered, but in short...		
• I am not sure how to put this, but I suppose generally speaking...		
• second conditional		
• ... I would	• possibly consider... (doing this) • maybe contemplate... (doing this) • maybe contemplate taking up... • perhaps reflect on... (doing this)	
expressing preference		
• As long as this happens, I'll do this.		
• Provided that there are no..., I'll head off to...		
• Unless there's..., I'll be making my way to...		
• On condition that it's not..., this... will be my destination		
• Supposing that I was .., I would head off to do this...		
• Say that I no longer had this..., I would probably do this		
discussing the benefits		
• The good thing about this is I'll be able to do this sooner than expected		
• The major advantage is I may not have to do this		
• One of the strengths is I'll have more time to prepare before I do this		
• One of the merits is I'll have more time to prepare before I do this		
• On the plus side I may do this		
• The beauty of this is I can have this		
• One of the added benefits is this		
mentioning the drawbacks		
• On the downside...	• The bad thing about this is I may not have this • The main disadvantage this • One of the weaknesses is I may not have this • One of the shortcomings is I may not have this	

Table 17. Summary of the possible question types that may be aroused during the first part of the Speaking Test general answers

Question	Answer
Description • What is this like? • How is this? • What does this look like? • How do you like this? • Can you describe this?	• Actually, to be fair, I would like to begin by stating that there are several points I could make. The first thing I should mention is that... Another point I would like to bring to your attention is... which is a second feature of it. Furthermore, I suppose I should underline the fact that... As a final point which may have escaped your notice, in addition to what I have just said, if times permits,...
like/dislike • Do you like... ?	• As a matter of fact, I guess that generally speaking I would certainly say that I am quite fond of... I simply adore... (it) and in particular... I suppose the reason has something to do with the fact that...
Frequency • How often do you do something? • Where do you usually do something? • When do you do something? • At what time of the day do you usually do something? • Who do you spend your free time with?	• Let me think. I imagine that it would depend on the situation. To be more exact,... While on the other hand...
Yes and No • Do you think doing this is better than doing that? • Will you do this if you do that? • Have you been doing this for long? • Did you like this? • Are there any interesting... ?	• So, to start with, I suppose to some extend..., in particular if you think about the point that... However, at the same time, you also have to consider that... So, all things considered, I reckon that the answer probably would have to be both yes and no.
Hypothesize • Would you like to do this? • Would you like to be this? • What do you do if you have this? • What will you do if this is like that then? • What would you do if you did that? • What would you have done if you hadn't done this/that?	• Well to be honest, I am not sure how to put it. I do not think I have ever thought about that, but in short, I imagine, generally speaking, I would possibly consider... (doing this). Provided that there is no... (if I had the power to change things), I would do this. (**or** Supposing I were/was... I would head off to... do this). One of the merits doing so, is... On the downside, one of the weaknesses is...

In this stage the first Examiner introduces the topic of the speaking task and provides instructions for the rest of the Test. Actually, this Stage is where the long, four-stage decision making task begins.

Each student is given a sheet of paper with notes about two of the four options. You read your own notes and do not look at the other candidate's notes. You have enough time to quietly read your information sheet and learn what your options are, prepare yourself a) to summarize them, b) to make a recommendation to your partner, and c) to silently choose one of your own options as the best.

After having read the points through quietly, you and the candidate describe your two options in turns. The first candidate presents his/her two options to the second candidate by summarizing the information given. While the first candidate is doing this, the second one should think which option is better. When the first candidate has finished summarizing, asks his/her partner to express an initial opinion about which of the two options is better. The second candidate recommends one of the two options and explains why. The first candidate chooses which option is better, but does not express it yet. Next, the candidates change roles and the second candidate repeats the same procedure with his/her notes.

When candidates are listening to their partner's descriptions note-taking is permitted. You can take notes if you wish to, but it might be or might not be surely helpful, as you need to be familiar with doing it (taking notes). On the other hand, if your partner is taking notes, you need to look at him/her and make sure he or she can keep up with you. The candidate who is taking notes would briefly interrupt the other candidate using appropriate language if there is a point that he/she didn't manage to write down (*Table 5*). In case you did not take notes and you do not remember everything that is said in your partner's description, do not worry. Besides, you do not have to remember anything that was said! Your task is to evaluate what is being said and recommend which of the two options is better. Apart from that, asking questions about what has been said is an effective way to keep the conversation going and make a good impression to the examiner.

Now, some advice about what to say in your presentation:

- One of the criteria that examiners will assess you on is your ability to ***summarize*** the bullet points under each option. To do this well, you need to be able to read the points quickly, fix the main ideas in your head, and then tell your partner about them in your own words. Although you are asked to paraphrase or summarize, really you need to elaborate. Usually, this involves saying why an advantage is indeed advantageous (or the opposite). A good piece of advice is to sort out the points into three categories: a) facts that simply describe the options; b) points in favor; and c) points against. Write a plus next to the benefits, a minus next to the drawbacks, and a circle next to the facts. This way you will be able to introduce your options with the most appropriate language. Start your summary with a topic sentence, including comments about what you are going to say, and go on with a series of phrases based on the bullet points.

- When you finish, ask your partner to comment on.

- The most common way to make a *suggestion* in English is to use either *should* (if you think something is really a good idea) or *could* (if you are just talking about one possible suggestion). You could add the words maybe or perhaps (more formal) to your suggestion to alleviate it. To easily communicate your meaning when making a suggestion, and also show your English ability to the examiner, use the expressions shown in *Table 18* so that your suggestion appears more organized and fluent.

- The examiners will also assess your ability to explain the reasons behind your decision. When you give your opinion about your partner's options, briefly give a reason by just highlighting the biggest advantage of the preferred option.

- After having made your recommendation take the initiative to move the conversation on, saying that it is now your turn to present the other two options.

- At the end of this section the examiner will probably ask you to state which of your two options you prefer. You shouldn't give any reasons for your choice at this stage.

Table 18. Summarizing and elaborating options, and recommending best option with main justification

Summarizing options

- According to the information I've been given, the second option offers...
- My notes say that... which I think...
- Of the two options I was given, the first one is... / the second one is about...
- Another argument in favor of/against... is...
- On the other hand,...
- One benefit/ drawback is that...
- Well, to begin with,...
- What's more,...

Elaborating option

- **A** is different from **B** in that the former is a...
- Apart from these,...
- Besides,...
- Moreover,... Furthermore,... What is also mentioned here is that... Last but not least,...
- On the one hand, there is... On the other hand, the...
- There are three main reasons for... For one thing,... For another,... Finally,...
- Well, the point I'm trying to make is that...
- While there is a need for..., the... still prefers to... (do this).

Recommending

- I highly recommend you doing this.
- I would strongly advise against doing this.
- If you want my advice, you ought to do this.
- No matter what, you have to do this.
- On no account should you do this.
- Take my advice: do this.
- You would be well-advised to do this.

Suggesting best option

- After hearing about both options, I think I would choose... because...
- As far as I can see, the first...
- I really feel that... is preferable because...
- I really think that... is preferable because...
- I recommend choosing X instead of Y because...
- I think this problem could be solved by choosing
- I think what should be done is...
- I think you should...
- I would have to suggest... for the position of... because...
- I'd advise you to choose X because...
- I'd suggest that you choose X over Y since...
- If I had the power to change things, I would...
- If I were you, I would choose...
- If you ask me... is the best option because...

In Stage III the two candidates have to come to an agreement on one single option. They begin this stage by announcing their final choices (which of their own options each one prefers), and then they discuss them in order to come to a common agreement about which one they will finally recommend. They should do this by comparing and contrasting the choices they have made, discussing the advantages and disadvantages of both options, and presenting counterarguments to support them. They should not look at each other's notes yet.

It is mandatory that you, the two candidates, come to an agreement on a single option. You are not expected to persuade your partner that your option is the better one. So, don't simply reject your partner's point of view. Instead, respond to your partner's comments. Your task is not to fight for your option and pressurize your partner into agreeing that yours is best. You will need to explain the advantages of your choice and the disadvantages of the choice that you have decided against.

As it has already been said, you are supposed to reach an agreement. You cannot agree that you disagree. In these cases, one of you should take the initiative and suggest that it's time to reach a conclusion.

As you need to have come to a consensus about one of the options within five minutes, avoid arguing too long, but also avoid coming to a consensus too quickly. Even if you think your partner's option is the best, spend some time talking about the strengths of your chosen option.

If you disagree with your partner's final choice, it's OK to try one last time to change his/her mind. But if your efforts fail be diplomatic and allow Stage III to end by accepting your partner's decision as graciously as you can.

As one of the things examiners are looking for in this stage is your ability to understand what has been said previously and to build on it, the first part of Stage III is an important opportunity for you to demonstrate the full range of your communicative skills. So, in order to perform well, don't begin with a long speech in defense of your chosen option. Instead, refer back to your partner's recommendation from Stage II and then go on to agree or disagree with it, using a sequence of appropriate phrases to introduce your own justifications and elaborations. Moreover, use questions as they help to keep the conversation going back and forth. When you finish speaking, after having analyzed your two choices (yours and your partner's, invite your partner to comment on your ideas (use phrases from *Table 19*). Similarly, when you begin each new turn, it's a good idea to acknowledge what your partner has just said with a polite phrase of agreement or disagreement.

Keep your discussion focused on the task in hand. You have to make a decision in an imaginary situation. Explore or highlight the criteria that ought to be important for this particular situation and refer back to it from time to time.

If you made notes in Stage III, you can refer to them in this Stage. However, if you didn't make notes and there is an important point that you can't remember, it doesn't matter. Ask your partner about it, as questions are more impressive in interview (actually, it might be beneficial to have a few gaps in your memory, though artificially).

In English, telling people how you feel about something they have just said requires a bit of finesse. You have to be able to say what you want without offending the other person using a lot of polite expressions in your speech. Frankness is something that English speakers do not necessarily appreciate. Therefore, it would be more preferable to express your **agreement** and **disagreement** using polite phrases (***Table 18***) instead of direct ones.

Table 19. Phrases that can be used to express agreement and disagreement

Express agreement	
• Absolutely! Personally, I would like to..., it sounds really... (e.g. exciting)	• Quite right. And another thing that must be borne in mind is...
• Good idea	• Quite right. And I would also like to add that...
• Hm, you've got a point there. Perhaps, I should...	• That is exactly what I had in my mind
• I agree entirely	• That's a good idea. We can...
• I am with you 100% on this one	• That's a good point
• I completely agree	• That's exactly what I think
• I hadn't thought of it like that	• That's just what I was thinking
• I have to say that I totally agree/ disagree	• That's really a valid point
• I suppose so	• That's what I want to say
• I tend to agree with you	• There is no doubt about it
• I think so	• We see eye to eye
• I think you have an interesting point	• Yeah, I'd go along with that
• I totally agree with you	• Yes, exactly
• I understand what you are saying. Of course, we should... since...	• Yes, I agree
• I was just going to say that	• Yes, I thoroughly agree. I also think it would be a good idea to...
• I whole-heartedly agree	• You are absolutely right
• I would go along with that	• You are right. It is possible that...
• I'd go along with you on that	• You have a point there
	• You have my support on this one
	• You took the words right out of my mouth

Table 19. Phrases that can be used to express agreement and disagreement

Express disagreement/present counterargument	
• I agree that's the downside, but...	• I understand what you are saying, but...
• I agree up to a point but...	• I'm afraid I'm going to have to differ
• I agree with you to some extent, but I think...	• I'm not absolutely/totally/fully convinced that...
• I am afraid I can't accept that point of view	• I'm not at all sure that/whether...
• I am afraid I can't accept your point of view	• I'm not sure I quite agree with you on that
• I am afraid I cannot agree with you when you said...	• I'm not sure I'll go along with you on that
• I am afraid I have to disagree with you...	• I'm not sure that's a good idea
• I am afraid that...	• I'm uncertain whether...
• I am not sure I quite agree...	• In a sense, however,... It is worth checking out, I suppose
• I am sorry that is unacceptable for me	• Isn't it possible that... ?
• I am sorry, but I really can't agree with you on that	• It must be said that..., however,...
• I am sorry, I have to disagree with you...	• It sounds interesting, but...
• I can't agree with you as...	• On the one hand..., but on the other hand,...
• I can't say I agree with you because we should also bear in mind that...	• Perhaps, don't you think that... ?
• I can't say I have very strong views either way	• That is not how I see it. As one problem with that option is...
• I completely/partially agree/don't agree at all with... because...	• That's not always the case
• I don't know for certain, but I think...	• That's true up to a point, but...
• I don't think it would be advisable to...	• To tell you the truth, I have very strong reservations about...
• I don't think there is any need to...	• We don't see eye to eye
• I doubt whether...	• Well, to be honest, I do not think...
• I honestly don't see why...	• Well, to be quite honest...
• I see what you mean, but...	• What will happen if... ?
• I see your point but I can't agree with you on that	• With all due respect, I have to disagree
• I take your point but...	• Yes, but on the other hand...
• I tend to disagree with you	• Yes, but you've got to remember that...
• I think you are not right	• You are mistaken
• I totally disagree with you	• You may be right, but let's not forget that...

Table 19. Phrases that can be used to express agreement and disagreement

Partly agreeing	
• I agree in principle, but... • I agree up to a point, but... • I agree with you on the whole, but... • I agree, though I would imagine that it would be difficult to... • I don't completely agree you on that • I'd tend to agree with you on that • That's very true, although I am not sure... • To a certain extent I agree with you, but...	• To a certain extent/degree... Well, I can't argue with that, but I should imagine it's quite... (stressful) • Well, you have a point here, but... • Yes, maybe but don't you think it would be a good idea to... ? • Yes, you are quite right and... • You may say so, but...

Politely disagreeing	
• Do not forget that..., so that... might not be a good idea • I am not certain that... • I am uncertain about... • I can't agree with you as... • I do not think it is necessary to... • I have doubts about... • I know what you mean, but... • I still feel that... • I understand what you are saying, but I think you are mistaken • I wish I could, but... • I'm sorry, I have to disagree with you there. If it is not pointed out,... • It sounds good in theory, but I am not sure it would work in practice. I mean you have not taken... into consideration, have you?	• Lets' see. I think... might be more suitable... • Maybe, but bear in mind that... • Maybe, but bear in mind that... • Not really, the way I see it,... • OK, so how about... ? • Possibly, but I reckon... • Possibly, but I reckon... • Well, to be honest, I don't think... • Yes that is a possibility, but do not you think it might be better... • Yes, I see your point. However, in my opinion it is nearly impossible to... Is it not better to... than... ? • Yes, that's a possibility, but don't you think it might be better to... ? • You are right, but...

Insisting on a point	Summarizing the decision
• I don't think we should dismiss this... • I think this deserves careful consideration • There's a lot to be said for... • I still think... would be more appropriate • I still think our first idea was the best	• So which one do we feel is best:... or... ? • So have we decided that... ? • So, from what we've both been saying, I think it's fair to say that we agree on X as the best choice. Do you agree? • I'd say that... Do you agree?

Suggesting	
• After hearing both options, I think we would choose... because...	• It makes sense to choose... because... It might be a good idea to...
• Besides, I wouldn't recommend... since...	• Might it be an idea to...
• I really feel that... is preferable because...	• Of the two, I'm inclined to believe... would be a more suitable choice because...
• I really think that... is preferable because...	• Of the two,... is definitely more suitable because...
• I recommend choosing X instead of Y because...	• Of the two,... would be an excellent choice because...
• I think this problem could be solved by doing this	• To solve this problem, I think we should...
• I think we should...	• Well, in my opinion it's more important that... although I do see your point about...
• I think what should be done is...	
• I was wondering if you'd ever thought of...	• What is more,... would be an inappropriate choice, as...
• I'd suggest that we choose X over Y since...	• What is more... would not be a good choice, as...
• I'm convinced... is the ideal... (option) for... seeing that...	• Why don't we... ?
• In my opinion,... definitely isn't cut out for... (e.g. the position of) because...	

Stating preferences	Suggesting an alternative
• As far as I'm concerned, the best...	• Generally speaking, the second idea...
• From my point of view, the best...	• I partly agree with your proposal, but...
• Given the choice, I would have to say this	• I see what you mean up to a point, but...
• I'd go for this one because...	• I'm not absolutely convinced that... is the best choice, since...
• I'd much prefer that one because...	• Let's look at something else
• I'd rather have that one because...	• Not to be taken lightly is the fact that...
• If I had to take a pick, I'd favor for doing this, as you can enjoy that	• Of course we could always...
• If I had to take a pick, I'd go for doing this, as you can enjoy that	• Something worth mentioning is...
• This one is preferable because...	• The first idea has a lot in its favor, as it...
	• There is also the matter of...
	• There is another option
	• What about... instead?

Table 19. Phrases that can be used to express agreement and disagreement

Expressing doubt	
• I take/see your point but... • I see what you mean but... • I agree with you on the whole but... • But don't you think/see that... ?	• That's true I suppose but... • That's an interesting point of view/comment but... • Well, you have a point there but... • Might it not also be true that... ?

Arguing/Elaborating	
• ..., while/whereas... • Although there are obvious advantages to..., its disadvantages/drawbacks/downside should not be neglected. • In spite of/Despite... • It is clear that... is the more appropriate choice, mostly because... • My notes say that... is..., which I believe shows that... • One other advantage is that... • That is all well and good, but there are... who... on the grounds that... • The benefits of... are... but the challenges are... • The disadvantage is... • The first... (option) has a lot of positive qualities, such as...	• The main advantage of... is that... • The main strength of... is that... • The weakness is... • There are both advantages and disadvantages to/in... • There are both positive side and negative side to... • There are two sides in this issue. On the one hand,... On the other hand,... • Well, I am in favour of... because... • Well, I feel that one of the main advantages of... is that... • While there are obvious advantages to..., its disadvantages/drawbacks/downside should not be neglected.

Reaching a consensus	
• I can't argue with that. So, what we are saying is that... will be more beneficial to.., however,... • I do see your point. Let's go with that one! • I respect your opinion, of course. However, the basic question is which... will benefit more by... • I wouldn't recommend... since... • It would seem to me that... is the better choice, mostly because... • So basically, we can't seem to agree on which... to choose • That is right. To sum up, I think... is/are... and... is/are... While you think...	• I think we can accept your opinion on that • Well, I do not think that it is such a good idea because... • Well, I think it would be a good idea to..., don't you? • Well,..., of course, but we seem to be in complete disagreement on the issue of... • Yes I think we can both agree on that. • Yes, I see what you mean, but shouldn't we also consider that... ? • Yes, I suppose you're right. I'll go along with your choice, then • Yes, that's definitely an advantage • Yes, you're probably right about that.

Table 19. Phrases that can be used to express agreement and disagreement

isn't/aren't/won't... and... isn't/aren't/won't... • That's a good point • Unfortunately, there are some disadvantages to... such as... However, on the downside,... would be a problem as...	That's a very good point, actually, and I believe... • Yes, you're probably right about that. That's a very good point, actually • You're right. I hadn't thought about that • You've got a point there

Introducing Examples	
• A called **SO** is a classic example of this • A called **SO** is a fine example of this • A called **SO** is a prime example of this • A called **SO** is a typical example of this • A case in point is this • A classic example of this is... • A fine example of this is... • A prime example of this is... • A typical example of this is... • Actually, I think this idea is best illustrated with an example of... • Additionally, another major cause for concern has to be the fact that... • As a matter of fact, this point can be demonstrated with the case of... • Especially,... • Essentially, one fundamental concern is probably that... • For example,... • For instance,... • In actual fact, this notion can be confirmed by the example of...	• In fact, this concept can be illustrated by the example of... • In one case, there was a... (specific reference on something) which did this • In particular,... • In some instances **As** actually have a higher What(?) than **Bs** • Let me give an example... • One example of this is... • Particularly,... • Take this for example, it doesn't even have that • Take... as an example/instance. • There are many As which are just as... (adjective e.g. popular) as Bs..., to name a few (used when giving many examples) • There's no better example than this, which... • This is shown by the fact that... • To illustrate this point, let us consider...

In Stage IV you, the candidates, formally present your common choice to the second examiner stating reasons in order to convince him/her that the option you have chosen is the best one. In the first 2-3 minutes of this stage you should collaborate in order to prepare a formal and well-organized presentation which will be made to the second examiner.

Before making the presentation, you have to plan what you will say clarifying which the four strongest reasons for your final option are chosen from those that have already been discussed and are presented in the information sheet. You also may invent or add new points by expanding on the points you chose and elaborating the information given in the information sheet. In any case, it would be good to briefly write these four points you are going to make to persuade the examiner that your jointly chosen option really is the best. Do not consider any negative point at this stage. Instead, prepare your arguments to refute the possibly aroused criticism.

Each of you must be able to present one (1) point and two (2) different reasons that have led to your final choice, explaining why these reasons are important. Having clarified the four reasons, you must quickly decide how to allocate them so that each of you presents two reasons. As the examiners are listening and assessing your performance, do not forget to take turns and build on what your partner says. By writing down which points will be presented by you and which by your partner will help avoid you ending up with little to say because your partner accidentally covers one of your points. It is worth noting that it is only in this stage that you can look at each other's information sheets.

Having decided who will say what and in which order, you must turn to the examiner and announce to him/her that you are ready, using appropriate language, and present your allocated points as persuasively as possible, ignoring the fact that he/she has already heard everything. In any case, don't skip the introductory comment which connects logically the previous with the present stage. If you speak first, find a way to pass the presentation over (hand over) to your partner. Don't just stop speaking and expect him/her to jump in. Finally, if you are the second to speak, conclude the presentation using proper wording. Remember to avoid any informal language as the presentation is supposed to be rather formal.

In this Stage, the second Examiner questions you and your partner about the decision you have made and presented in Stage IV. The purpose of this stage is not to challenge your choice, but rather see how well you can defend it by justifying the reasons that lead to your decision and by exploring it in more detail.

The second examiner asks questions or makes comments on the option you presented in Stage IV and the reasons you gave. You have to justify and defend your chosen option by expanding on the points you have mentioned. You must be prepared to be asked about the possible drawbacks (at least one negative point or disadvantage) of the option you recommended. In your presentation in Stage IV you will have highlighted four advantages without having mentioned any drawbacks of the chosen option. In this Stage the examiner will probably want to find out about a weakness or failing you didn't mention. At least one of the second Examiner's questions will focus on any problem areas your option may have. He/she might convey the impression that he/she thinks your choice was the wrong one. Do not worry; he/she is obliged to say something against your choice just to keep the conversation going. The examiner may raise the negative point about your option and you should refute this criticism appropriately. You need to be able to defend your choice by saying that this drawback is not so serious and explain why. You revisit both sides of the argument, refer to and build on things you probably said previously. Your comments to the second Examiner will sound more formal and persuasive if you begin by acknowledging what he/she said and then politely build on saying whether you agree or disagree. Lastly, you could pass a few things over to your partner using appropriate language (*Table 20*). This gives you a good opportunity to use concession language and grammatical structures that are impressively complex. Remember that there are no right answers and that you are only asked to develop your reasoning.

As this is the first time that the second Examiner will speak to you, you'll need to get used to his/her voice without the benefit of a warm-up phase. If you miss something, don't hesitate to ask the examiner to repeat or clarify what was said using phrases from *Table 8*. The second Examiner usually plays the role of someone in authority (e.g., the director of a company or the principal of a school), so use language that is slightly more formal and polite than what you may have used with your partner.

Giving/Expressing opinions	
• ... is a good case in point. I can give you one example of it • A lot of people think that... but I think... • As far as I am concerned... • As far as I can see,... • As far as I can tell... • As far as I'm concerned, everyone should have the opportunity to do this so that they can do that • As far as I'm concerned,... • As for me,... • As I see it,... • Don't you agree that... ? • For me personally,.. • Frankly, I think... • From my point of view, I think... • I am convinced that... • I am of the opinion that this contributes a lot to this • I believe/think/feel that... • I feel... • I find... particularly upsetting/ worrying/disturbing because... • I have no doubt that... • I strongly believe doing this is necessary, especially for them • I strongly/firmly believe that... • I think governments need to introduce far stricter controls on... As far as I know... • I think the most effective solution would be to... • I think this is a priority because... • I would say that... • I would say that... • I'd like to point out that... • I'm not sure about this, but I would guess that... • I'm quite sure that... • I'm strongly opposed to...	• In my view, the problem of... is the most serious, as... One way to prevent it would be to... • In my view,... • It seems to me that... • It seems/appears to me... • It's (quite) clear (to me) that... • It's hard to say, but I imagine I would advise her to... • It's obvious that... • Let me give you an example • My first thoughts on this are (that)... • My initial reaction is... • On the whole, I'm (not) in favour of... • One way to approach this might be to... • Personally speaking,... • Personally, I feel that... In this way, if... should... • Personally, I feel... is a great way of... • Personally, I think... • Personally/Frankly I think that... • Speaking from personal experience,... • The first thing I should say is... • The first thing I would do is to... • The other thing I should say is... • The way I look at it... • This is just my opinion, but... • To be honest with you, I am certain that... • To be honest with you, I am sure that... • To be honest, I think... • To my mind this is adventurous and exciting, especially when you are still young • To my mind... • To tell you the truth, I (firmly) believe/ think that... • To the best of my knowledge, doing this is only affordable to them... • To the best of my knowledge...

- If I were to choose one of these..., I'd go with... because...
- If you ask me doing this is only beneficial as... but as... as well
- If you ask me...
- In my experience, doing this helped me become a more open-minded individual
- In my opinion, doing this offers that...
- Well, as far as I'm concerned, I'm of the opinion that...
- Well, I think there are... reasons:...
- Well, it is common sense that...
- Well, the main reasons I think include...
- What I think is that...
- What I think is this:...

Giving Reasons

- A third, and perhaps more important reason, is...
- All the same, the downsides of this cannot be ignored
- Alternatively, these can also do that
- And finally, the deciding factor for us was...
- Another equally important reason...
- Another important reason is ..,
- Being/Having... also makes this a good option.
- But the deciding factor for us is that...
- Despite/In spite of these obvious benefits, the dangers cannot be ignored
- Even so, this does not always live up to expectations
- First and foremost,...
- First of all,... Then there is the issue of...
- Firstly... Secondly...
- Having said that, this does have a lot to answer for in terms of this
- I would also like to point out that...
- I would put it down to the fact that it's so...
- In addition to... there is also the fact that...
- It should also be taken into consideration that...
- It's all thanks to...
- On the other hand, these can still offer as much this as this can
- One advantage of... is... Another is...
- The beauty of... is that it makes you feel like you... In comparison, other... What's more,... are just a few great... All in all, if...
- The main point in favor of...
- The main reason is . . .
- The reason behind this is the fact that...
- There are several reasons for our choice.
- There can be no doubt that... is...
- Therefore, we strongly believe...
- This is good for... whereas the other one is still a much safer... option
- This is why we have decided . . .
- To begin with, we would like to highlight the fact that..,
- We believe that the best proposal is...
- We shouldn't forget that... You should bear in mind that if...
- We would attribute it to the fact that I...
- What convinced us that... was more suitable was...
- What makes it a cut above other... to mention but a few of the... it offers. A direct result of being/having such a thorough and detailed... is... (e.g. people) will... Then again, I must admit...

Table 20. Useful phrases for justifying and defending opinions

Dealing with doubts and objections – Refuting	
• At first, we were also concerned about that, but it doesn't really matter	• That concerned us as well. We realize it is not a perfect solution, but...
• I just don't see the logic behind..., especially if one takes into consideration that...	• That's a valid concern, which of course we did take into account. Our feeling, however, is that, although... no longer... (do this), it is important for them to...
• I see no harm in...	
• I think I've covered everything	• That's an interesting question
• I think you raise an important issue, but having weighed the alternatives, we are convinced that...	• That's certainly one way to look at the situation, but it must also be argued that...
• I would say this statement is rather simplistic/too extreme/absolutely true. For example...	• This may seem impossible/improbable to you but...
• I've never really thought about that before, but I would say...	• We discussed that point
• It adds another interesting angle	• We don't think that this poses a problem
• Look at it in another way...	• We feel this point is something than can be overlooked because...
• So bearing that in mind,... seems an obvious choice	• We gave that problem some thought and decided that...
• Taking into account that..., it/he/she is clearly the best option	• What you are suggesting definitely has validity. It's true that..., but one also needs to consider...
• While this has a lot to offer, there is nothing like doing this	• You needn't worry about...

Announcing the common choice
• Our decision is...
• My partner and I have decided that... would be the best choice as...
• We are convinced that X is the best option

Giving a result
• The end result is that somebody will have..., as no one will ever be...
• This is/are the product/result of...
• The need for... this arises/stems/comes from the fact that...

Pinpointing the reference (to the second Examiner)	Closing your presentation
• You mentioned...	• To sum up...
• Could I go back to the point you made about... ?	• For all the reasons we have given. We believe the proposal for a... is by far the best.
• I was interested in your comments on...	
• You stated that...	• Last but not least, I would like to say that...

5. The end of the Speaking Test

The examiner will conclude the Speaking Test, letting you know that it has come to an end, by saying something appropriate, like wishing you good luck and saying goodbye. ***Table 21*** presents some common expressions and the most possible responses to them.

Table 21. Useful phrases for justifying and defending opinions	
Examiner's expressions	**Candidate's responds** (Expressions you could use)
• Well, that's the end of your interview. Thank you. • It's been very interesting talking to you.	• Goodbye. It's been nice talking to you. Bye. • I enjoyed talking with you. Goodbye. • I really enjoyed talking with you. • It has been very helpful talking to you. • Nice talking to you. • Thank you for your time. • Thank you for your time. Goodbye. • Thank you very much for your help. • Thank you. • You have been very helpful. Goodbye.

PART II

A GENERAL MODEL OF THE SPEAKING TEST

Despite of the fact that controversial topic discussions like juvenile crime, the role of the media, or the degradation of the environment are not included in the new form of the ECPE Speaking Test there is a considerable number of potential topics that could be discussed in Speaking Test (e.g the vacancy for a science teacher). Therefore, it is important not to reduce speaking preparation to an absolute minimum duration in the belief that it can be practiced and honed in an intensive fashion over a two- or three-week period towards the end of the course.

However, instead of making a huge list of topics and practicing them it is easier to put them into similar groups or categories. One of the obvious advantages of such an approach is that there is a common vocabulary for each group and hence the candidate can focus its learning attempts on the appropriate type of language, not on separate responses to every possible topic. In most cases, it is possible to use the same content and grammar for many different topics. Nevertheless, it is important to try to learn sophisticated and uncommon vocabulary for each topic area.

The answers provided in this part of the book are only some of the possible ones that may be given. They contain complex grammar structures and sentences, linking words and phrases and redundant language. Depending on the pace of speaking it will take you at least half the time provided to speak in the Test. That is the reason why it is very helpful using them as a method of answering. Depending on the topic you only have to find content to cover the elapsed time.

Main Steps/Actions of the Speaking Test in appearance order

1. Greetings (begin/end)
2. Introduce yourself
3. Answer general questions about yourself
4. Answer general questions about the topic
5. Summarize the two options: facts, points in favor/against
6. Take notes
7. Make recommendation/suggestion and give reasons explaining why (highlight the strongest advantage)
8. Describe/Summarize/Elaborate the selected option
9. Discuss the advantages and disadvantages of both options, compare and contrast them
10. Express opinion
11. Collaboration and Planning of a short conversation
12. Announce your final choice
13. Move on the conversation
    - invite your partner to present his/her part
    - Invite your partner to comment on your ideas/to carry on the conversation
    - Invite your partner to take part in the conversation
    - Refer back to your partner's recommendation
14. Present counterarguments
15. Agree on a single option
16. Plan what you will say
17. Select four strong reasons and clarify them
18. Allocate the reasons between you
19. Decide who will say what and in which order
20. Announce the examiner that you are ready
21. Present comment which connects logically the previous with the present stage
22. Present your allocated part
23. Pass the presentation over to your partner
24. Refer back to your partner's part
25. Present your allocated part
26. Conclude the presentation using proper wording
27. You will be asked about the possible drawbacks/negative point of your choice
28. Refute this criticism by revisit both sides of the argument. Begin by acknowledging what the examiner said. Defend your choice.
29. Pass a few things over to your partner.

Stage I: Introduction/Breaking the ice - Small Talk (3-5 minutes)

(At this stage you will be asked non-sensitive, tactual background information (e.g. family, school, occupation, hobbies) or questions relating to the theme of the speaking task.)

First Examiner: Hello, my name is... and I'd like to ask you to spend a few minutes getting to know each other.

(or
Let's start by getting to know each other a bit)

See Table 9

First Examiner: Since the task you are going to do is about..., I'd like to start by asking you some questions about...

These questions are hard to be foreseen. Use the methodology presented in the previous chapters and summarized in table 17.

Stage II: Presenting, Summarizing and Recommending (5-7 minutes)

(In this stage the topic of the speaking task will be introduced and instructions will be provided.)

First Examiner: O.K. Now let's move on to Stage II and let me introduce you to the topic under discussion.

You have been asked by... to serve on... to select the most suitable...

Here is some information about the four final... (1) been considered.

Each of you will receive (/have/be given) information (/a sheet with brief notes) concerning two different (/about only two of the) options about the... (1)

You will have 2-3 minutes to look at the information you are given. When you're ready, one of you will describe your two... (1), to your partner using your own words and provide as much detail as you can, based on the information you have been given. At the same time, the other one will be listening and then in the end be asked to express (/give) his(/her) opinion about(/on) (say which he/she prefers) who(/which of the two he/she thinks is more suitable for/satisfies the criteria for/ deserves to be selected as/be awarded the)...

You do not need to memorize anything, as you may look at your sheet at any time, but you are not allowed to look at your partner's sheet.

If you wish you may take notes, but there is no need since you are free at any time to ask your partner to repeat or clarify any of the information he(/she) is presenting.

Then you will switch roles. In the end, you will have to narrow your choices down to one of the four and present it to the... (e.g the school principal, the committee).

If you have any questions about the instructions, please feel free to ask. (The first Examiner hands out information sheets.)

[The first Examiner listens while candidate A presents their choices and candidate B makes recommendation, Then both candidates switch roles: candidate B presents and candidate A recommends]

– Shall I start first?

– Yes. Sure!

– Well, to begin with of the two options I am given the first one... is...

*... **See Table 22***

Well those are my two options... (partner's name), which do you think is better?

– Well, after hearing about both options (e.g. candidates), I think that the first/second one..., is really worth considering as... This is mainly because I believe that... should be given priority when it comes to...

Let me now continue with the presentation of my two options (e.g.

candidates). According to the information I have been given, the first candidate/option... is...

... See Table 22

I think that is all I can tell you about my two options. Now, what do you think of them?

– Well, taking everything you said into account, my opinion is that it is a very difficult choice. Nevertheless, since I have to single out one, I would give emphasis to... (some feature, e.g. someone's need) for... (e.g. financial aid) and propose... The reason is he(/she/it/they) is(/are)...

First Examiner: Now I'd like you to take a minute or two to decide silently which of your own two... (1) you think is better(/is better for... /is better suited for... /is best/deserves the)...
Remember that either (1) is good, but you need to select only one. When you are ready, we will move on to Stage III.

[The first Examiner is silent while candidates are taking their time to think]

Stage III: Consensus Reaching (5-7 minutes)

(Candidates are still not allowed to look at each other's notes)

First Examiner: Now for Stage III. I'd like you to work with your partner and take turns reporting to each other which... (1) (option) you chose.

– Now I would like to continue with my final choice between... and... In the last phase you recommended me... and I have to say that I totally agree. I think you were right about... As I see it, I believe it was easy to distinguish... from... and he(/she/it/they) should receive(/be selected as)... All things considered, that's why I have decided on...

– I agree with you. Now as far as my two options (e.g. candidates) are concerned, I am finding it difficult to choose between them. Therefore, I will make it easier by adopting your advice and decide on... After all, he(/she/it/they) is... and certainly deserve(s) to be... (given/selected as). Well, that's my opinion and the reason for it.

or

–Despite what ... (partner's name) recommended (/suggested) in the last phase, I feel strongly that... would be a better choice. Although... has some good features such as... and..., it seems to me that... would provide a more valuable... to... I say this because... So for all these reasons, I think...

First Examiner: *Now, at this stage, you will have to cooperate and narrow your choices down to one out of the two.*

You need to contrast and compare your choices (requesting and supplying information, negotiating and providing reasons, discussing the advantages and disadvantages of each), your choice with the one your partner has selected, and come to an agreement as to (until you agree on) the option that you think is the best(/whose is better... (1)/which... (1) is the best/which... (1) should get the grant/which... (1) you think)...
Your goal is to choose the best option. Remember that either option is good, but you need to select only one. You also need to give the reasons for your final decision and explain why they are important. Remember that you are not allowed to look at each other's sheet.

– So, well, why don't we start by looking at the advantages of each option and decide on the best course of action narrowing our choices to one, the best option for our case.

– Good Idea. Shall I start?

– Sure. Go for it and tell me why you think your preferred option is the one we should really recommend. What is your most important reason?

Option A. Not coming to agreement from the beginning

– Well, to begin with, I believe that... would worth being taken into account when deciding on... To illustrate this point, let us consider... On this basis, I would recommend choosing... for... How do you feel about this?

– You certainly have a point there. After all,... is... and... And with regards to..., maybe the fact that... makes it difficult for... to... However, on the other hand, as far as my chosen option is concerned, I think it is a good case in point as well. Actually, I think the reason why it is preferable could be best illustrated with the example of... Do you agree or disagree?

– Probably, I can see what you mean up to a point. In this case,... would definitely be of great help(/beneficial). However, I am not absolutely convinced that... is the best choice, since... Can I have your input on this?

– I do not know for certain, but I think that in a sense,... is worth checking out. I think... deservers careful consideration, as I still believe it/he/she would be a more appropriate choice for... What are your thoughts on this?

– I agree with you to some extent, in spite of the fact that it is not how I see it, as there are some problems with that option. Nevertheless, to tell you the truth, I do not have very strong reservation about... and as we have to proceed with a common choice I think we can accept your opinion on that. So, let us go with that one. Do you agree?

– You are right! I had not thought about that this way. Let us go on.
Option B. Coming to agreement from the beginning

– Well, to begin with, I believe that... would worth being taken into account when deciding on... To illustrate this point, let us consider... On this basis, I would recommend choosing... for... How do you feel about this?

– You certainly have a point there. After all,... is... and... And with regards to..., maybe the fact that... makes it difficult for... to... I think your opinion is right.

– I am glad you agree with me. Apart from what I have also mentioned, I recommend choosing my option instead of yours because to me what also counts is... Therefore, it is my opinion that... should get selected as... What do you think?

– I agree entirely. Actually, that is just what I was thinking. Of the two options,... would be an excellent choice for... because... Do you agree with me?

– Absolutely! I totally agree with you. However, do not you think your preferred option needs being considered? I think it has at least some positive aspects, too.

– I am not sure I quite agree with you. Of these options, I am inclined to believe... would be a more suitable choice for... What convinced me that this is the proper proposal to make is that...

– So, we have decided that... is our final choice. All right?

– That is right! Let us go with that one.

Option C. Partner reluctant to speak and in need of help

– Well, to begin with, I believe that... would worth being taken into account when deciding on... To illustrate this point, let us consider... On this basis, I would recommend choosing... for... How do you feel about this?

– I suppose so. I would say I agree with you. Hmm, I have no idea where to begin. Any ideas?

– Well. Which feature of your chosen option do you think deserves to be mentioned so that it could be considered a good solution?

– Ok. I think... is an important factor that makes my option to stand out.

– I think you are right, but to be honest, I consider my choice the most suitable as... Have you any hesitation on that?

– No. You are probably right about that. That's a very good point actually and I believe... as well.

– Well, in addition, I reckon... is definitely an advantage. So, it would seem to me that... is the better choice, mostly because... What do you think?

– Yes. I suppose you are right. I will go along with your choice, then.

– So, we have decided that... is our final choice. All right?

– That is right!

Option D. Coming to agreement after discussion

– Well, to begin with, I believe that... would worth being taken into account when deciding on... To illustrate this point, let us consider... On this basis, I would recommend choosing my option for... How do you feel about this?

– I think you have a point there. However, I believe that my option deserves to be considered, too. The main reason is... And another important reason is... What is your opinion?

– You are right. To tell you the truth, I believe that both options, yours and mine, are strong candidates. Under these circumstances, if you agree, I propose to select that option which best satisfies the needs of... So, which one do you think is the most suitable solution?
– Well, a good... (candidate) for... ought to have... Therefore, I think we should choose... In addition, he (/she/it/they) is (/are/has/have)... which makes him (/her/it/them) the ideal option for our case.

– So, from what we have been saying, I think it is fair to say that we agree on... as the best option. This is our final choice. Do you agree?

– Yes, that is exactly what I had in my mind. Let us go with that one.

Stage IV: Presenting and Convincing (5-7 minutes)

(At this stage, Candidates formally present their final decision to the second Examiner. They are now allowed to share the sheet containing the information concerning their final choice while collaborating with each other IN ENGLISH to prepare a convincing presentation)

First Examiner*: O.K. this is fine. In the final stage, you are asked to formally present your decision to... (2) (/to the second Examiner who plays the role of... (2)) and persuade him/her that the choice you've made is the best.*
[The first Examiner introduces the second Examiner to Candidate A and Candidate B]

I'll give you 2-3 minutes to plan what you will say (/your presentation and which reasons you will each present). You must convince him/her that your choice is the best.
You may at this point read each other's sheet. You must each present two different reasons and explain why they are important justifying your choice. When you are done (/After your presentation),.... (2) will ask you some questions.
[Candidates prepare a presentation of their recommendation and decide on the reasons each will

– So, what features do you think we should focus on?

– Well, I think we should start with the fact that... and also... do you agree? (1st reason)

– Absolutely, I can see your point. Furthermore, I think that... is an also important factor which could back up our choice. Can you think of anything else? (2nd reason)

– Well, coming back to the aim of this process, which is to propose the most suitable... (candidate/trip/project/...) for... having... (this particular feature/need/our school reputation) in our mind, I reckon that referring to... would strengthen our choice. (3rd reason)

– I guess you are right! So far we have three reasons and we only need one more to have a complete and rational reasoning. (*or in case your partner has referred to two instead of only one reason you could respond saying something like this:* I think you have mentioned two reasons, namely... and... Combined with what I have already said we have three reasons and we only need one more to have a complete and rational reasoning). Having this in mind, I think we should attribute our decision to the fact that this option offers another important benefit to... In other words... This can be deemed as the fourth reason of our choice. What do you think?

– I think that we have enough reasons to justify our proposal. However, what about defending the negative aspects? What will we say about... ?

– I think you raised an important issue, but if we weigh the advantages of our option we can back it up and convince the... (e.g. committee/principal) as well

– What are you suggesting definitely has validity. It is true that..., but what someone needs to consider is that it does not matter as... is more important.

– It adds another interesting angle. However, I reckon that it is enough with it. What about the other options? Why did we eliminate them?

– Well, while they may have a lot to offer(/they would deserve to be selected for...), there is nothing like... So, I do not think that they pose any problem.

– Before we proceed with the announcement of our final decision, I reckon it would be advisable to allocate the reasons having led to it between us so as no one covers the same points as the other or someone been left with nothing to say.

– I agree entirely. That is what I wanted to point out (/ I was just going to say that).

– I think I should present the first two positive aspects and you can talk about the rest ones. What do you think?

– It sounds fair. Shall I start first?

– Sure. Go ahead!

– Well, we are ready to present our chosen option.

Second Examiner*: Hello. My name is... and I am
ready to listen to your choice.*

– After a lot of thought and discussion my partner and me have finally decided that... would be the best choice as... we (/he/she/it/they) will have the greatest benefit for/from... Actually, all four options (e.g. candidates) seemed to be excellent candidacies (e.g. personalities). However, we both agreed that in the first place, emphasis and priority should be given to... On these grounds we eliminated the other options (e.g. candidates). Apart from this, there are four other main reasons why we believe our choice is right. To begin with, the first reason, although not the most important, is that... We say this because... We also believe that...

Those are two of our four justifications. My partner has another two, don't you... (Partner's name)?

– That's right! Thank you for your introduction. In addition to what... (Partner's name) already mentioned, I would also like to point out that our final choice was based on... (e.g. the candidates' financial situation), which tipped the scales in favor of... And finally, and perhaps the most deciding factor for us was... To recapitulate, our final choice is... and is based on the reasoning we just presented. For all these reasons we believe our proposal is by far the best.

[When they finish their presentation the second Examiner begins last stage.]
Second Examiner*: Now I'd like to ask you a few questions to make sure I understand your decision.*
Are you realty sure we should be... (doing this)? After all, now that...

I understand, but what do you have to say about the fact that... ? Isn't this a disadvantage?

– You mentioned that... I would admit that I certainly agree with you. This is a valid concern, which of course we did take into account and gave that problem some thought. However, we focused on... and decided that... because of... This was another reason that convinced us that... is the best option and deserved to be... (selected/awarded the... /proposed for...).

Second Examiner*: This may be true. What is also true though is that at least two of the other candidates are certainly worth choosing if we take a closer look at their qualifications. For example...*

– You stated that... which is a good case in point. You are definitely right. And that's the reason why we found it very difficult to make a choice. At first, that concerned us as well and we gave it some thought. But we realized that we are not seeking for the perfect solution. So, the fact that... doesn't really matter and you needn't worry about it.

(The second Examiner closes the speaking test and thanks the candidates for their presentation)

Second Examiner*: Well, all right then. I'd like to thank you both for your input. We'll be sure to take your comments into account when we make our final decision. Thank you for your time and you are free to go.*

Respond using appropriate phrases from ***Table 9***.

(1)
apartment(s)
candidate(s)
college(s)
course(s)
facility (ies)
language course(s)
option(s)
people
project(s)

(2)
the director
the director of the National Park
the head of the committee
the person in charge of... in the city council.
the president of the Council.
the president of the Parent Teacher Association
the school's headmaster.
your friend who is planning to...
your neighbor

Your Task	To select one student who will receive the Student of the Year award

Option 1 — **According to the information provided the first candidate is** *Benjamin Button*. He was voted the smartest student of his class, **which means that apart from** being intelligent, he is deeply appreciated by his fellow students, as well as by his teachers. **This also accounts for why** he is seen as an outgoing and popular person. **In addition, he is a very active person, as he participates in a lot of activities such as** being a member of the school chess club. Actually, he is the person who founded and runs it. **As far as his grades are concerned**, he is a top student, **since** his grades are remarkably high, **especially in** science and math. **Furthermore,** he comes from a lower class family, **meaning that** he may have financial problems and consequently he may not have the ability to support himself in case he wants to pursue further education in college. **However, on the other hand, a negative aspect of this candidacy is that** he is overconfident and arrogant, **which means that he might not be the right role model for other students**.

Option 2 — **Now let me turn to the second option, the second candidate, which is** *Natalie Fox*. She is not only the top student in her class, **being both** studious and serious **when it comes to** studying, **but also** a highly gifted musician. **It is worth mentioning that** she works part-time to pay for music lessons **as** she also comes from a lower class family. **This means that she has to** devote more effort studying the rest of her time. **Nevertheless,** her financial state has not deprived her of winning a national song-writing competition. **Not surprising since** she is hardworking and enthusiastic. **The fact that** she loves music **is the reason why** she wants to impart her knowledge to underprivileged children by giving free guitar lessons at the junior high school and by helping in organizing local community music concerts. **Finally, the fact that** she skips classes frequently **could be seen as a drawback of** her. **However,** hers overall performance and her dedication **could overcome this minor flaw**.

PART III

PRACTICE AND EXERCISES

A. As it has been stated in the corresponding chapter, after greetings, the examiner will begin by asking the candidates some very general and simple questions about themselves (e.g. about their family, where they come from, their home town, their studies, their likes and dislikes, their hobbies, or what their interests are, etc.), the so called "getting-to-know-you" questions, which will help him/her find out a little about them. Then the examiner asks the candidates non-sensitive, factual background information (such as school/work/occupation, family/friends, hobbies/interests/leisure activities, plans for future vacation/travel, reasons for taking the Proficiency exam, and ambitions) (*Table 10*) or starts a conversation on one or more general topics related to the theme of the speaking task (*Table 11*). These questions are a warm-up to the rest of the test. The possible questions are innumerable. Nevertheless, it is possible to predict the most frequent and to prepare yourself for them. This way you will be able to answer these questions properly and correspond to any other possible question successfully. Complete *Table 22* by answering those questions that are suitable for your case. Not all questions are applicable to all candidates. For example, you either work or study. It is not usual in our (western) society to work while studying for your first degree, or while in school.

Do not try to give an exact answer to the question presented in *Table 22* providing absolutely accurate information. It is meaningless. Instead, you should give an extended answer that demonstrates your ability to understand the question answered and your English knowledge. Therefore, answer the question included in this *Table* considering these as group questions. Use the language presented in *Tables 12-16* and the model answer contained in *Table 17*. Keep in mind: there is no right or wrong answer. On the contrary, there are only correctly or wrongly formulated answers.

Table 22. Possible "getting-to-know-you" and topic related questions

Possible Questions	Your answers
You	
• What is your name?	
• Could you tell me your name please?	
Family	
• Could you tell me something about yourself/your family?	
• How old are you?	
• Do you live by yourself or with your family/your parents?	
• Do you have any brothers or sisters/ siblings?	
• Are you married or single?	
• Would you like to live in a big family?	
• Do you like going out with your family or with your friends?	
Living place	
• Can you tell me where you are from?	
• Where do you come from?	
• Where are you from?	
• Where did you grow up?	
• Where were you brought up?	
• Where did you spend your childhood?	
• What about your own childhood?	
• Where do you live?	
• Can you describe where you live (your city/home town/village)?	

Table 22. Possible "getting-to-know-you" and topic related questions	
Possible Questions	**Your answers**
• Have you always lived there? • How long have you lived there? • Have you ever lived in any other place?	
• What kind of city is your home town? • Is it an attractive/pleasant place for visitors? • Is it known for anything in particular? • Does your city have any historical importance? Are there any historic monuments there? • Are there any interesting places to see?	
• What could a visitor see/do when they visit your home town? • What areas in your city or region would you recommend tourists visit and why? • What are the main tourist attractions in your home town? • If I visited your city, what would you advise me to go and see? • What can visitors do there? / What is there to see?	

Possible Questions	Your answers
• Do you like living in your home town? • What do you like about the area where you live (your town)? • Would you like to move to a bigger area? • Would you like to be inhabitant of a small village? • Do you like living in the centre of a big city? • Do you think it is better to live in the center of a town or in the countryside? Why?	
• What are some of the problems of urban life? • What do you find difficult about living in your home town? • Are there any advantages of living where you are at present? What are they?	
• What kind of place are you living in at the moment? • Is it easy to find accommodation in your home town? • Do you (or your parents) own your house?	

Table 22. Possible "getting-to-know-you" and topic related questions

Possible Questions	Your answers
• Can you describe the house where you live? • Can you describe your study room/bedroom?	
• What changes have taken place in your city in recent years? • How do you think your city could be improved?	
• What types of restaurants are there in your city/town? • Do you like shopping? How are the shopping centers in your home town? • What do most teenagers like doing in your town?	

Table 22. Possible "getting-to-know-you" and topic related questions

Possible Questions	Your answers
Education/Study	
• Are you working or studying at the moment?	
• Have you graduated or are you still studying?	
• Are you studying now?	
• Can/Could you tell me something about your education/educational background?	
• What are you studying?	
• What was/is your major?	
• What did you major in?	
• What's your field of study?	
• Describe the course you are studying?	
• Which subject did you study at university?	
• Have you got any other diplomas or degrees?	
• What do you like about it/about your studies?	
• Why did you choose that subject?	
• What do you most dislike about your study/course?	
• What do you find most interesting about your school's courses?	
• What is your favorite subject?	

Table 22. Possible "getting-to-know-you" and topic related questions	
Possible Questions	**Your answers**
<ul><li>What languages can you speak?</li><li>How often do you use English?</li><li>What is the reason you are taking this exam?</li><li>Why are you learning English?</li><li>Why is English important to your future?</li><li>What made you choose a Proficiency course?</li><li>What do you need the certificate of Proficiency for?</li><li>How useful will it be in the future?</li><li>What do you need the certificate of Proficiency for?</li><li>How long have you been studying English?</li><li></li><li>Have you ever done a research? What was your research on?</li><li></li><li>Have you ever won a university scholarship?</li></ul>	

Possible Questions	Your answers
• Have you ever attended a summer course?	
Job	
• Are you working at the moment? • Tell me about the work you do. • What do you do for a living? • What's your job? • What kind of jobs are you good at?	
• What are some of your main responsibilities/your work routine? • What are your duties? • What does your job/work involve? • What exactly are your duties as... ? • Can you describe one of your typical working days?	

Possible Questions	Your answers
<ul><li>What is your ideal job?</li><li>What would your dream job be?</li><li>Which careers really interest you?</li><li>What (things) do you like/enjoy about your job? Why?</li><li>What gives you job satisfaction?</li><li>What do you find difficult in your job?</li><li>Why/When did you choose this job/ to do this job?</li></ul>	
Future plans	
<ul><li>What are your plans for the future?</li><li>Do you have any ambitions?</li><li>What are your ambitions?</li><li>How easy or hard will it be to achieve those ambitions?</li><li>What's your biggest ambition in life?</li><li>What would you like to be doing in ten years' time?</li><li>Where do you see yourself in ten years' time?</li></ul>	

Table 22. Possible "getting-to-know-you" and topic related questions

Possible Questions	Your answers
<ul><li>Are you willing to keep your job permanently?</li><li>Do you want to change your current job? Why or why not?</li><li>Apart from work, what other ambitions do you have?</li></ul>	
<ul><li>What are your future plans after graduation?</li><li>What plans do you have after you graduate your current school?</li><li>What subject would you like to study at university?</li><li>What do you hope to do after your graduation?</li><li>Where would you like to study; at a university where you could live at home or at a university where you would live in a dormitory or apartment and come/go home only infrequently?</li></ul>	

Table 22. Possible "getting-to-know-you" and topic related questions	
Possible Questions	**Your answers**
Hobby/Free Time	
• How much free time do you have at the moment?	
• How do you spend your free/leisure/spare time?	
• What do you like/enjoy doing in your spare/free time?	
• How do you usually spend your free time?	
• Have you got a hobby? If so, what is it?	
• What hobby would you like to take up?	
• What kind of hobbies or leisure time activities are you interested in?	
• What indoor activities do you enjoy?	
• What games/sports do you play/do?	
• What games/sports are you good at?	
• Why do you like doing these activities/about your hobby?	
• Are you able to make time in your schedule to play sports or get regular exercise?	

Table 22. Possible "getting-to-know-you" and topic related questions	
Possible Questions	**Your answers**
• What do you usually do at weekends? • Do you prefer going to the cinema or theatre? • Who's your favorite actor/actress? Why? • Are there any special places you like going to when you go out?	
• Which do you prefer: eating in restaurants or eating at home? • Which are the best places to eat out?	
• How important is it to have adventure in our lives?	

Table 22. Possible "getting-to-know-you" and topic related questions

Possible Questions	Your answers
Holidays/Traveling	
• Have you ever been abroad? • What other countries have you visited? • What interesting places have you visited? • Are there any countries you would like to visit?	
• What kind of holidays do you prefer? • If you could have holiday anywhere in the world, where would you go? Why? • Would you like to have a sightseeing holiday? Where?	
• Do you like travelling? • How would you like to travel around? • What do you find interesting/difficult about travelling?	

Table 22. Possible "getting-to-know-you" and topic related questions

Possible Questions	Your answers
• Would you prefer to stay in a hotel or rent an apartment? • Which kind of hotels do you prefer?	
Shopping	
• Do you enjoy going shopping? Why (not)? • How much time do you spend shopping every week? • What is your favorite shopping centre and why do you like it?	
• What problems are there with shopping in your area? • What things do young people like to buy? • What can shops do to make shopping more pleasant for their customers? • Do you think that in the future people will do most of their shopping using the Internet? Why?/Why not?	

Possible Questions	Your answers
Reading	
• Do you enjoy reading? Why? • What sort of things do you read? • Do you think it is important for people to read a lot? Why (not)? • What is your favorite book? • What are the advantages of reading instead of watching television or going to the cinema?	
Environment	
• Why is it important to protect nature? • In what ways is nature in danger? • Do you think people are overly concerned about protecting the environment these days or do you think there is real cause for people to be worried? • In terms of local problems, what do you think people in your area are most concerned about? And why? • What role could an individual play in terms of doing something to protect the environment?	

Table 22. Possible "getting-to-know-you" and topic related questions

Table 22. Possible "getting-to-know-you" and topic related questions

Possible Questions	Your answers
Cultural heritage	
• Why are historic buildings and monuments important to a city? • Is it better to keep old buildings, or build new modern ones? • What museums does your hometown have?	
Pets	
• Have you ever held a pet? • Do you have any pets? • If not, would you like to have any? Why? Why not? • Do you see yourself owning a pet in the future? • If so, who took care of the pet? Was it you or someone else in your family? • If not could you explain why not? • What are some of the advantages or disadvantages of pet ownership for families with children?	

Table 22. Possible "getting-to-know-you" and topic related questions

Possible Questions	Your answers
Public transport	
• How do you think public transport could be improved? • Do you think people should use public transport more? Why (not)?	
Other issues	
• If you could make one change in the health care system of your country, what would it be?	

My daughter is a nurse and she works in the local hospital. In the past she used to work for an international health care company. On the other hand, my wife runs a small traditional resort hotel in a nearby village and my brother manages a gift shop downtown.

I am in charge of a small company. In particular, I am responsible for a group of workers in the sales department. Every day, I have to deal with clients' complaints and mainly overseas clients using computers a lot of the time. Apart from this, I have to go/attend (to) a lot of meetings/ sales conferences, visit/see/meet clients and when coming back I advise my coworkers how to work more effectively by giving them any help they need. Fortunately, it does not involve writing letters or filling in forms or doing any other paperwork, as I have a secretary responsible for all these.

I have a full-time job, but I am not a workaholic. I would like to be on flexi-time so that I can enjoy my time the way I like. In the past I used to work part-time/have a part-time job, however, I was forced to do/work overtime in order to be able to cope with my financial needs. Nevertheless, I was made redundant even though I had a lot of experience in this area and was trying to be hardworking and work efficiently. That time it did matter, as I meant to give up work in order to continue my studies and got a temporary job working in an accountant office. I was employed as a secretary assistant for a couple of months. It wasn't my field, I would like to specialize in family law.

Now, I'm quite competent and efficient at my current job as I am sufficiently qualified for this position. Efficiency is very important in this kind of work. Furthermore, as it is a demanding job the fact that there is a great teamwork helps get the job done on time. Sometimes, we need to team up with another group to finish our project. We usually cooperate with European firms on that kind of projects.

It is not easy to get/find work in small cities related to writing, but I would love to do this kind of work even if it is difficult to make a living as a freelance writer.

Bringing up/raising children is never easy, but I am trying to give them a good upbringing.
We're identical twins. We closely resemble/really take after our mother. On the other hand, my brother bears a remarkable resemblance to my father. You can easily see the resemblance between him and my father.

My wife and me are both native of a small city, named... which is a picturesque town especially in the spring. There are a lot of historic buildings. However, we left our home town to study in another bigger town and after our marriage we set up house there. It is a city of 100,000 inhabitants/citizens. Despite the fact that we used to live on the outskirts of the city and now we moved downtown, we have a pretty hectic social life, got used to the better standard of living provided in this city and we no more fell homesickness. In big towns, you can see a continual bustle of people coming and going.

As in most big cities, there is a commercial centre and, combined with the fact that many people live in the suburbs and have to travel to work in the centre of the town, everyday, particularly in the rush-hour, we are/get often stuck in a traffic jam. The streets get so packed with traffic that travel is very slow or even comes to a standstill. This is really stressful for commuters who travel to work in the town. Apart from this, homelessness, as well as vandalism, are some of the major problems in inner-city areas especially of big cities resulting in growing concern.

For these reasons, it is not difficult to understand why some people prefer the countryside to big towns. They often say that towns are noisy, dirty and polluted, stressful, and crowded; while, the countryside is quiet and peaceful, clean, calm and relaxing. In addition, it has lots of open space. On the other hand, those who still prefer big cities maintain a different point of view. They say that in towns there are plenty of things to do, and life is exciting. Moreover, there is a wide range of shops and lots of night-life. On the contrary, in the countryside, there is nothing to do; it's boring. There are only a few shops and no night-life. Thus (= That is why) a lot of people are moving out of rural areas to urban areas.

I am a university student and got a place at Aristotle University of Thessaloniki, in the department of psychology. I'm doing an undergraduate course and this time I have to start revising for my exams as soon as possible since any delay will result in losing vital time, since like all the students I have to hand in a research paper or an essay; time is money. Furthermore, I need to do well in my assignment as well as in the exam. After graduation, I am planning to spend a year abroad before I do a postgraduate degree. I'm hoping to get a student grant or to win a scholarship, to be able to deepen my study by getting a MSc (Master of Science) without distraction stemmed from financial issues.

I've got a degree (BSc – Bachelor of Science) {*Or alternatively: I'm a graduate (a person who holds a (first) degree from a university) in, or I graduated (receive an academic degree or diploma) in ... from ... [University]*} in Environmental Science and now I'm majoring in Air Pollution. I am doing some research into how pollution can affect human behavior. I have already done a preliminary study of the subject. I have gathered data on air pollution sources, as well as I have collected a lot of statistics relating to air pollution and human well-being. Data collection has already been finished and I am doing the analysis now. At the moment, I am at the final phase of my PhD writing my thesis. However, I still have to test the theory by experiment. There are a lot of people with expertise in this field. My dissertation is being supervised by a well-known professor who carried out/performed a series of significant experiments to test his theory, which I am expanding now.

I have joined a club so I can go camping in the summer with other people. In the past I used to do a bit of/a lot of climbing and hiking. I took up hiking when I was at the first year of university because I wanted to get more exercise, but I gave it up three months ago and now I usually go jogging two or three times a week. Furthermore, I like photography, I am mad about DIY (Do It Yourself) and I try to practice playing the guitar.

I'm doing my garden, just for fun. However, I think I get more pleasure out of learning Italian than anything else as there isn't much entertainment for young people in this town.

I am a great traveler. That is why I have been to every part in my country. Last year, my wife and I toured/went/were on a tour round the Northern Europe. We travelled overland to Paris and stopped off in (made a stopover at) Napoli en route/on the way to Rome. We had the time of our lives. My wife wants now to go on an excursion to the mountains, but I prefer going cruising in the Mediterranean. So I decided to book two weeks in Crete in July to combine both desires. The island's economy is heavily dependent on tourism. One of the most famous landmarks in Crete is Knossos. We had a great time last year, so we decided to repeat it.

B. In this section, same traits that can be used to characterize an option of the speaking task are listed. Use your words to paraphrase and elaborate them according to the particular information the task prompt may contain, or imply. Complete ***Table 23***.

Table 23. Paraphrasing and elaborating traits associated with a option of the speaking task

Task: Recommend	Trait	Paraphrase and Elaboration
A		
the best candidate for school president	• Class president	
	• Founded and runs school environmental group	
	• Active member of debating society	
	• Sets very high standards	
	• Confident when speaking in public	
	• Good reputation with students and teachers	
	• Straight-A student	
	• Not a team player. Doesn't share ideas with other people	

Table 23. Paraphrasing and elaborating traits associated with a option of the speaking task

Task: Recommend	Trait	Paraphrase and Elaboration
B		
a coach for the local sports centre	• His students have a 100% success rate	
	• Gives free music lessons at the junior high school	
	• Male, Age 25	
	• Elementary school gym teacher at a private school (2 years)	
	• Is a recent graduate	
	• Winner of a youth triathlon	
	• Available only during evenings and weekends and unavailable in afternoons	
	• Not so good at working under pressure	

Table 23. Paraphrasing and elaborating traits associated with a option of the speaking task

Task: Recommend	Trait	Paraphrase and Elaboration
C		
one student who will receive the Student of the Year award	• Captain of school debating team	
	• Member of various volunteer groups	
	• Sets very high standards	
	• Dedicated to any commitment she makes	
	• Held in high regard by teachers	
	• Second highest grade in school	
	• Emphasis on continuous improvement	
	• A bit distant and reserved	

Table 23. Paraphrasing and elaborating traits associated with a option of the speaking task

Task: Recommend	Trait	Paraphrase and Elaboration
D		
an advertising agency for a campaign encouraging young people to stay healthy	• Company set up four years ago	
	• Young, enthusiastic team	
	• Produces imaginative computer and graphic animation	
	• Won awards for previous campaigns	
	• Very reasonable prices	
	• Guarantees never to go over budget	
	• Never done a health-related campaign	
	• Ads tend to be quite futuristic in design	

Table 23. Paraphrasing and elaborating traits associated with a option of the speaking task

Task: Recommend	Trait	Paraphrase and Elaboration
E		
how to spend a sum of money to contribute to a worthy cause	• Last school gym renovation done 25 years ago	
	• Gym classes recently reduced from 3 times a week to once a week	
	• Add new weight room and climbing wall	
	• Helps disabled students to train	
	• Demolition of some space necessary	
	• Permission needed from town council	
	• Would require closing gym to students for an entire year	
	• Public highly critical of proposed restrictions (Local citizens cannot make use of it, only students)	

Table 23. Paraphrasing and elaborating traits associated with a option of the speaking task		
Task: Recommend	**Trait**	**Paraphrase and Elaboration**
F		
the best science trip for your class	• Visit animal sanctuary	
	• Field Trip to a Forest	
	• Learn about endangered species	
	• Two days and one night	
	• A 4 hour flight and an 1-hour bus ride	
	• Excellent food, variety of dishes	
	• $450 per student	
	• Only for students with passports	

Table 23. Paraphrasing and elaborating traits associated with a option of the speaking task		
Task: Recommend	**Trait**	**Paraphrase and Elaboration**
G		
possible locations for the next Olympic Games	• Excellent stadiums and sports facilities	
	• Cosmopolitan population	
	• Large international airport	
	• All accommodation within walking distance of the sports centers	
	• Beautiful historical sites	
	• Not too expensive	
	• Cooler weather	
	• Not enough accommodation facilities	

Table 23. Paraphrasing and elaborating traits associated with a option of the speaking task

Task: Recommend	Trait	Paraphrase and Elaboration
H		
a city site to be restored	• Building with many representations and symbolism	
	• To be demolished if not restored	
	• Needs major repairs	
	• Costs about $30,000. Quite expensive	
	• Partly government subsidized	
	• Some private donations available	
	• May bring glory to the city and increase tourism to the area	
	• Public highly critical of appropriate restrictions during reconstruction works	

Table 23. Paraphrasing and elaborating traits associated with a option of the speaking task

Task: Recommend	Trait	Paraphrase and Elaboration
a shelter dog to be adopted as a gift for your 10-years old cousin	• 18 months	
	• Sit, stay on command	
	• Neglected by previous owner	
	• Long black coat	
	• Nervous around strangers	
	• Shedding a problem; needs frequent brushing	
	• Friendly, very active, gentle giant	
	• Could reach 60-70 kg fully grown	

Table 23. Paraphrasing and elaborating traits associated with a option of the speaking task

Task: Recommend	Trait	Paraphrase and Elaboration
J		
the most suitable Colleges for the son of a friend of yours	• Prestigious historic college on edge of a big city with lots of culture	
	• Ranked 15th on list of top 50 small colleges	
	• 1 hour from home	
	• 30,000 undergraduate students	
	• 25 Students per Class (seminars + some lectures)	
	• $12.000 a year Tuition Cost	
	• Offering a full tuition scholarship to Honor students	
	• Dormitory close to many attractions (museums, galleries, shopping)	

C. Now, using the methodology presented in the previous chapters of this book, write two paragraphs describing the two options given for each speaking prompt. (Give a full description of each option.)

The student council has asked you to serve on a committee to select the most suitable scholarship recipient. You have to decide among four options.

Candidate A

Option 1 (Tim Cross)	**Option 2 (Anny Parker)**
• Captain of school debating team	• Class president
• Active member of debating society	• Member of various volunteer groups
• Sets very high standards	• Deeply interested in science
• Confident when speaking in public	• Dedicated to any commitment she makes
• Good reputation with students	• Multiple projects done on time
• Overconfident and arrogant	• Doesn't have many friends

The first candidate/option whose details I have is

Now let me turn to the second candidate/option, which is

The student council has asked you to serve on a committee to select the most suitable scholarship recipient. You have to decide among four options.

Candidate B

Option 1 (Niki Lada)	**Option 2 (Helene Benz)**

- High scorer on high school basketball team
- Gives free music lessons at the junior high school
- Grades just above average
- Good attention to detail
- Held in high regard by teachers
- Good public relations skills

- Former state school award's winner
- Helps at a centre for children with learning difficulties
- Average grades, doesn't study much – could do better if she studied harder
- Enjoys being part of a team
- Works well with others
- Brightly dyed hair and face piercings

The first candidate/option whose details I have is

Now let me turn to the second candidate/option, which is

You are members of a company's hiring committee and have been asked to choose the most suitable New Director of their local Department. You have to decide among four options.

Candidate A

Option 1 (Jenny Pappa)

- Female, 29 years old
- Sets very high standards
- Has many ideas for future gadgets
- Written English weak
- 4 years' experience in same post
- Impatient with customers

Option 2 (Mark Taylor)

- Male, Age 25
- Wants change of career
- Has set up his own business
- Mastered English in the USA
- No practical experience as Director
- Known to be temperamental

According to the information I have been given, the first candidate/option is

Now let me turn to the second candidate/option, which is

You are members of a company's hiring committee and have been asked to choose the most suitable New Director of their local Department. You have to decide among four options.

Candidate B

Option 1 (Paul Maker)

- Male, 59 years old

- Increased the productivity in his department up to 20%

- Has travelled widely overseas

- No formal related to the position training

- Management position, World Bank (10 years)

- Doesn't share ideas with other people

Option 2 (Petra Lack)

- Female, 27 years old

- Founded and runs the institute Inventors for the Environment

- Is leader of a youth group

- Speaks English, German, French, Danish

- Hired 6 months ago

- Looks young enough for such a post

According to the information I have been given, the first candidate/option is

Now let me turn to the second candidate/option, which is

You have been asked by the local high school board to serve on committee to recommend the most suitable Basketball Coach. You have to decide among four options.

Candidate A

Option 1 (Otto Gift)

- Former state champion

- Member of school sports teams

- Male, 32 years old

- So busy that she is hard to find

- Degree in Physical Education

- Not very creative

Option 2 (Susana Male)

- High scorer on his school basketball team

- Helps at a centre for children with learning difficulties

- Female, Age 27

- Only available evenings

- No formal training

- Not reliable. Never punctual.

The first candidate/option whose details I have is

Now let me turn to the second candidate/option, which is

You have been asked by the local high school board to serve on committee to recommend the most suitable Basketball Coach. You have to decide among four options.

Candidate B

Option 1 (Billy Idol)	**Option 2 (Margaret Smith)**
• Black belt in judo	• Plays in a basketball league
• Wrote master's thesis on "Physical Education Modern Teaching Methods"	• No practical experience as a coach
• No absences or late arrivals	• Is a recent graduate
• Male, 30 years old	• Female, Age 22
• Knows how to get an idea across	• Good reputation with students
• Had argument in public with school head	• Not so good at working under pressure

The first candidate/option whose details I have is

Now let me turn to the second candidate/option, which is

You have been asked by the city's board to join a local committee to select an advertising agency for a campaign encouraging young people to pursue more active life. You have to decide among four options.

Candidate A

Option 1 (Greener's)	Option 2 (Action)
• Company set up four years ago	• Operating for over 20 years
• Young, enthusiastic team	• Small, family-run company
• Won awards for previous campaigns	• Guarantees never to go over budget
• Uses imaginative graphic animation	• Ads tend to be quite conservative
• Will be very economical	• Very expensive
• Never done a health-related campaign	• Done several similar campaigns

According to the information I have been given, the first candidate/option is

____

____

____

____

____

____

____

Now let me turn to the second candidate/option, which is

____

____

____

____

____

____

You have been asked by the city's board to join a local committee to select an advertising agency for a campaign encouraging young people to pursue more active life. You have to decide among four options.

Candidate B

Option 1 (All Done On Time)	**Option 2 (Never let you down)**
• Only been in business for two years	• In business for 10 years
• Little experience with youth market	• Highly qualified, experienced team
• Specialize in medical treatment	• Have similar campaigns for major international brands
• Reputation for sticking to deadlines	• Involve clients in creative process
• Cheapest agency on the market	• Very reasonable prices
• Winner of an Advertising Award	• Projects done on time

According to the information I have been given, the first candidate/option is

----

Now let me turn to the second candidate/option, which is

You have been asked by the local board to serve on a committee to select a city site to be restored. You have to decide among four options.

Candidate A

Option 1 (Old post)	**Option 2 (Old Train Station)**
• Needs renovation since 5 years' time	• About to close for lack of proper facilities
• Local citizens unwilling to participate	• Public highly critical of proposed design
• Two months duration	• Three months duration
• Faster service → more revenue	• More visitors → more revenue
• Very expensive $200.000	• Rational costs $120.000
• Considered a City's Heritage	• Will be an new commercial centre

The first candidate/option whose details I have is

Now let me turn to the second candidate/option, which is

You have been asked by the local board to serve on a committee to select a city site to be restored. You have to decide among four options.

Candidate B

Option 1 (Medieval Castle (part of it))

- Restore area now spoiled by crime and graffiti
- Create more comfortable, attractive walking areas
- Visitor numbers limited - only specialized science
- Very expensive $1.200.000
- Will increase tourism to the area
- May bring glory to the city

Option 2 (Central square)

- Plant new trees to provide shadow
- Not recommended to take place during high season
- Public highly critical of proposed restrictions
- Low cost $10.000
- Will reduce carbon footprint of citizens
- Increases the levels of air quality

The first candidate/option whose details I have is

Now let me turn to the second candidate/option, which is

You a travel agency that has been asked to book a one-month holiday for a family. You have to decide among four options.

Candidate A

| **Option 1 (New Island)** | **Option 2 (Mountain Excursion)** |

Option 1 (New Island)

- 4 hour flight and 1-hour bus ride
- Excellent food, variety of dishes
- Accommodation in various hotels
- Luxury building with many amenities
- A bit expensive
- Needs to have passports

Option 2 (Mountain Excursion)

- 4 hours by train
- Provide shops and supermarket
- Sleep in log cabins
- Bright and airy
- Will be very economical
- Not recommended for those with health issues

According to the information I have been given, the first candidate/option is

Now let me turn to the second candidate/option, which is

You a travel agency that has been asked to book a one-month holiday for a family. You have to decide among four options.

Candidate B

Option 1 (Savanna Trip)	**Option 2 (Sea Resort)**
• Dogs/Pets allowed	• Fully furnished luxurious 3 bedroom/2 bathroom apartment
• Relatively intact cultural site	• Beautiful historical sites (ancient port)
• Camping in nature preserved areas	• 5 star hotel within walking distance from the beach
• Not very expensive	• Affordable room prices (not food included)
• Quiet, rural atmosphere	• Cosmopolitan population
• Not suitable for infants	• Modern transportation facilities

According to the information I have been given, the first candidate/option is

Now let me turn to the second candidate/option, which is

Some friends of yours have asked you to propose a shelter dog to be adopted for their kids. You have to decide among four options.

Candidate A

Option 1 (Rocks)	**Option 2 (Baxi)**
• 18 months	• 3 years
• Small female (about 10 kg)	• Large male (about 50 kg)
• Star pupil at obedience school	• Needs some obedience training
• Neglected by previous owner	• Used to live on the streets
• Short black coat	• Long, red coat
• Nervous around strangers	• Fond of shoes

The first candidate/option whose details I have is

Now let me turn to the second candidate/option, which is

Some friends of yours have asked you to propose a shelter dog to be adopted for their kids. You have to decide among four options.

Candidate B

Option 1 (Rocky)	**Option 2 (Rantanplan)**

- Newborn
- Male (about 45 Kg when grows up)
- Needs a lot of care until age 1 year
- Obedience school a must
- Thick, curly white coat

- Loving, but overly playful

- 5 years old
- Male very large in size (65 Kg)
- Obedient
- Home guardian
- Its owner is not able to keep it any more

- Friendly with kids

The first candidate/option whose details I have is

Now let me turn to the second candidate/option, which is

The student council has asked you to serve on a committee to decide how to spend a $50,000 (Grant) on School Improvements. You have to decide among four options.

Candidate A

Option 1 (Science lab)	**Option 2 (New gym)**
• Complaints that lab not being used effectively	• Gym classes recently reduced from 3 times a week to once a week
• Purchase LCD projector for modeling experiments	• Renovate school gym (last done 25 years ago)
• Add 5 more computer stations (bringing total to 10)	• Add new weight room and climbing wall
• Install new sprinkler system and smoke alarms	• Install all new flooring; current floor unsafe
• Not too expensive: $10.000	• Costs: $25.000
• Duration 3½ months. Totally closed.	• Duration 1 year. Totally closed.

The first candidate/option whose details I have is

Now let me turn to the second candidate/option, which is

The student council has asked you to serve on a committee to decide how to spend a $50,000 (Grant) on School Improvements. You have to decide among four options.

Candidate B

Option 1 (Schoolyard)	**Option 2 (School decorating)**

Option 1 (Schoolyard)

- Plan trees, new basketball court
- Install two kiosks, trash and recycling bins
- Will improve school environment
- Costs: $3.000
- Duration 2½ months. Totally closed.
- Summer and autumn

Option 2 (School decorating)

- Altering exterior
- Add paintings with bright colors
- Students can chose the subjects
- Not too expensive: $5.000
- Duration 1½ months. Totally closed.
- Summer

The first candidate/option whose details I have is

Now let me turn to the second candidate/option, which is

Some friends of yours have asked you to propose the most suitable Colleges for their son. You have to decide among four options.

Candidate A

Option 1 (Imperial)	**Option 2 (King's)**
• 30,000 undergraduate students	• 9,000 undergraduate students
• Students per Class: 150 (mostly lectures)	• Students per Class: 15 (small seminars)
• Tuition Cost: $34,000 a year	• Tuition Cost: $12.000 a year
• Ranked 9th out of top 40 large universities	• Ranked 15th on list of top 50 small colleges
• Scholarship: $10,000 for the first year	• Offering a full tuition scholarship
• Situated at city's doorstep	• Located at city's center

According to the information I have been given, the first candidate/option is

Now let me turn to the second candidate/option, which is

Some friends of yours have asked you to propose the most suitable Colleges for their son. You have to decide among four options.

Candidate B

Option 1 (City's Academy)

- 1,000 undergraduate students

- Students per Class: 50 (lectures and seminars)

- Tuition Cost: $1,000 a year

- Ranked 88th out of top 100 tertiary schools of the country

- Not a university

- Accommodation facilities not available

Option 2 (ScieUni)

- 130,000 undergraduate students, 50,000 postgraduate students and 5,000 doctoral students

- Students per Class: 250 (only lectures)

- Tuition Cost: $50,000 a year

- Ranked 2nd in world

- Professional opportunities very high

- On-site cafeteria, restaurant

According to the information I have been given, the first candidate/option is

Now let me turn to the second candidate/option, which is

D. For each option presented in Tasks 1 you have to 4 formulate four (4) advantages and one (1) disadvantage. These should be used to persuade your partner or the examiner in favor of each option.

The student council has asked you to serve on a committee to select the most suitable scholarship recipient. You have to decide among four options.

Candidate A

Option 1 (Tim Cross)	**Option 2 (Anny Parker)**
• Captain of school debating team	• Class president
• Active member of debating society	• Member of various volunteer groups
• Sets very high standards	• Deeply interested in science
• Confident when speaking in public	• Dedicated to any commitment she makes
• Good reputation with students	• Multiple projects done on time
• Overconfident and arrogant	• Doesn't have many friends

Advantages

1.	1.
2.	2.
3.	3.
4.	4.

Disadvantage

The student council has asked you to serve on a committee to select the most suitable scholarship recipient. You have to decide among four options.

Candidate B

Option 1 (Niki Lada)	**Option 2 (Helene Benz)**
• High scorer on high school basketball team	• Former state school award's winner
• Gives free music lessons at the junior high school	• Helps at a centre for children with learning difficulties
• Grades just above average	• Average grades, doesn't study much – could do better if she studied harder
• Good attention to detail	• Enjoys being part of a team
• Held in high regard by teachers	• Works well with others
• Good public relations skills	• Brightly dyed hair and face piercings

Advantages

1.	1.
2.	2.
3.	3.
4.	4.

Disadvantage

You are members of a company's hiring committee and have been asked to choose the most suitable New Director of their local Department. You have to decide among four options.

Candidate A

Option 1 (Jenny Pappa)	Option 2 (Mark Taylor)
• Female, 29 years old	• Male, Age 25
• Sets very high standards	• Wants change of career
• Has many ideas for future gadgets	• Has set up his own business
• Written English weak	• Mastered English in the USA
• 4 years' experience in same post	• No practical experience as Director
• Impatient with customers	• Known to be temperamental

Advantages

1.	1.
2.	2.
3.	3.
4.	4.

Disadvantage

You are members of a company's hiring committee and have been asked to choose the most suitable New Director of their local Department. You have to decide among four options.

Candidate B

Option 1 (Paul Maker)	**Option 2 (Mark Taylor)**
• Male, 59 years old	• Male, Age 25
• Increased the productivity in his department up to 20%	• Wants change of career
• Has travelled widely overseas	• Has set up his own business
• No formal related to the position training	• Mastered English in the USA
• Management position, World Bank (10 years)	• No practical experience as Director
• Doesn't share ideas with other people	• Known to be temperamental

Advantages

1.	1.
2.	2.
3.	3.
4.	4.

Disadvantage

You have been asked by the local high school board to serve on committee to recommend the most suitable Basketball Coach. You have to decide among four options.

Candidate A

Option 1 (Otto Gift)	**Option 2 (Susana Male)**
• Former state champion	• High scorer on his school basketball team
• Member of school sports teams	• Helps at a centre for children with learning difficulties
• Male, 32 years old	• Female, Age 27
• So busy that she is hard to find	• Only available evenings
• Degree in Physical Education	• No formal training
• Not very creative	• Not reliable. Never punctual.

Advantages

1.	1.
2.	2.
3.	3.
4.	4.

Disadvantage

You have been asked by the local high school board to serve on committee to recommend the most suitable Basketball Coach. You have to decide among four options.

Candidate B

Option 1 (Billy Idol)	**Option 2 (Margaret Smith)**
• Black belt in judo	• Plays in a basketball league
• Wrote master's thesis on "Physical Education Modern Teaching Methods"	• No practical experience as a coach
• No absences or late arrivals	• Is a recent graduate
• Male, 30 years old	• Female, Age 22
• Knows how to get an idea across	• Good reputation with students
• Had argument in public with school head	• Not so good at working under pressure

Advantages

1.	1.
2.	2.
3.	3.
4.	4.

Disadvantage

Task 4

You have been asked by the city's board to join a local committee to select an advertising agency for a campaign encouraging young people to pursue more active life. You have to decide among four options.

Candidate A

Option 1 (Greener's)	**Option 2 (Action)**
• Company set up four years ago	• Operating for over 20 years
• Young, enthusiastic team	• Small, family-run company
• Won awards for previous campaigns	• Guarantees never to go over budget
• Uses imaginative graphic animation	• Ads tend to be quite conservative
• Will be very economical	• Very expensive
• Never done a health-related campaign	• Done several similar campaigns

Advantages

1.	1.
2.	2.
3.	3.
4.	4.

Disadvantage

You have been asked by the city's board to join a local committee to select an advertising agency for a campaign encouraging young people to pursue more active life. You have to decide among four options.

Candidate B

Option 1 (All Done On Time)

- Only been in business for two years
- Little experience with youth market
- Specialize in medical treatment

- Reputation for sticking to deadlines
- Cheapest agency on the market
- Winner of an Advertising Award

Option 2 (Never let you down)

- In business for 10 years
- Highly qualified, experienced team
- Have similar campaigns for major international brands
- Involve clients in creative process
- Very reasonable prices
- Projects done on time

Advantages

1.	1.
2.	2.
3.	3.
4.	4.

Disadvantage

E. For each option presented in Tasks 1 to 4 in section D give one compelling reason why it is a good option and defend any drawback it may have.

The student council has asked you to serve on a committee to select the most suitable scholarship recipient. You have to decide among four options.

Candidate A

Option 1 (Tim Cross)

- Captain of school debating team
- Active member of debating society
- Sets very high standards
- Confident when speaking in public
- Good reputation with students
- Overconfident and arrogant

Option 2 (Anny Parker)

- Class president
- Member of various volunteer groups
- Deeply interested in science
- Dedicated to any commitment she makes
- Multiple projects done on time
- Doesn't have many friends

Reason in favor of it as the best option

Defend your negative side of your option

**

The student council has asked you to serve on a committee to select the most suitable scholarship recipient. You have to decide among four options.

Candidate B

Option 1 (Niki Lada)	**Option 2 (Helene Benz)**
• High scorer on high school basketball team	• Former state school award's winner
• Gives free music lessons at the junior high school	• Helps at a centre for children with learning difficulties
• Grades just above average	• Average grades, doesn't study much – could do better if she studied harder
• Good attention to detail	• Enjoys being part of a team
• Held in high regard by teachers	• Works well with others
• Good public relations skills	• Brightly dyed hair and face piercings

Reason in favor of it as the best option

Defend your negative side of your option

You are members of a company's hiring committee and have been asked to choose the most suitable New Director of their local Department. You have to decide among four options.

Candidate A

Option 1 (Jenny Pappa)	Option 2 (Mark Taylor)
• Female, 29 years old	• Male, Age 25
• Sets very high standards	• Wants change of career
• Has many ideas for future gadgets	• Has set up his own business
• Written English weak	• Mastered English in the USA
• 4 years' experience in same post	• No practical experience as Director
• Impatient with customers	• Known to be temperamental

Reason in favor of it as the best option

Defend your negative side of your option

You are members of a company's hiring committee and have been asked to choose the most suitable New Director of their local Department. You have to decide among four options.

Candidate B

Option 1 (Paul Maker)	**Option 2 (Petra Lack)**
• Male, 59 years old	• Female, 27 years old
• Increased the productivity in his department up to 20%	• Founded and runs the institute Inventors for the Environment
• Has travelled widely overseas	• Is leader of a youth group
• No formal related to the position training	• Speaks English, German, French, Danish
• Management position, World Bank (10 years)	• Hired 6 months ago
• Doesn't share ideas with other people	• Looks young enough for such a post

Reason in favor of it as the best option

Defend your negative side of your option

You have been asked by the local high school board to serve on committee to recommend the most suitable Basketball Coach. You have to decide among four options.

Candidate A

Option 1 (Otto Gift)	Option 2 (Susana Male)
• Former state champion	• High scorer on his school basketball team
• Member of school sports teams	• Helps at a centre for children with learning difficulties
• Male, 32 years old	• Female, Age 27
• So busy that she is hard to find	• Only available evenings
• Degree in Physical Education	• No formal training
• Not very creative	• Not reliable. Never punctual.

Reason in favor of it as the best option

Defend your negative side of your option

You have been asked by the local high school board to serve on committee to recommend the most suitable Basketball Coach. You have to decide among four options.

Candidate B

Option 1 (Billy Idol)	**Option 2 (Margaret Smith)**
• Black belt in judo	• Plays in a basketball league
• Wrote master's thesis on "Physical Education Modern Teaching Methods"	• No practical experience as a coach
• No absences or late arrivals	• Is a recent graduate
• Male, 30 years old	• Female, Age 22
• Knows how to get an idea across	• Good reputation with students
• Had argument in public with school head	• Not so good at working under pressure

Reason in favor of it as the best option

Defend your negative side of your option

You have been asked by the city's board to join a local committee to select an advertising agency for a campaign encouraging young people to pursue more active life. You have to decide among four options.

Candidate A

Option 1 (Greener's)	Option 2 (Action)
• Company set up four years ago	• Operating for over 20 years
• Young, enthusiastic team	• Small, family-run company
• Won awards for previous campaigns	• Guarantees never to go over budget
• Uses imaginative graphic animation	• Ads tend to be quite conservative
• Will be very economical	• Very expensive
• Never done a health-related campaign	• Done several similar campaigns

Reason in favor of it as the best option

Defend your negative side of your option

You have been asked by the city's board to join a local committee to select an advertising agency for a campaign encouraging young people to pursue more active life. You have to decide among four options.

Candidate B

Option 1 (All Done On Time)	**Option 2 (Never let you down)**
• Only been in business for two years	• In business for 10 years
• Little experience with youth market	• Highly qualified, experienced team
• Specialize in medical treatment	• Have similar campaigns for major international brands
• Reputation for sticking to deadlines	• Involve clients in creative process
• Cheapest agency on the market	• Very reasonable prices
• Winner of an Advertising Award	• Projects done on time

Reason in favor of it as the best option

Defend your negative side of your option

G. The following is a typical example of ECPE speaking Test. Using all previously presented information instructions and examples try to complete a full Speaking Test and create your own Model Speaking Test. Start by summarizing the information presented in this card and then find the most important advantages of each candidate. Use a blue pen to write the general part of the dialogue that does not change much among the different topics and red-ink pen to write the topic related part of it. Write a hypothetical dialogue covering your potential partner's responses, by answering not only the questions concerning your part but also his or her part. Try to imagine how he/she could react and prepare an appropriate reply. Be helpful to your partner and engage him/her in the conversation. This way you will be able to respond in any topic no matter how challenging it may be.

Shape your model response. Choose the way that fits your most and develop it. Any Speaking Test can be dealt with in the same way by you. No matter if you have answered all the preparatory Speaking Test the same way. During the examination procedure, you are expected to respond to only one topic. No one can find out that you use the same language to deal with and expand any topic. After all, it is really true that almost every subject can be developed in similar patterns. Finally, it is vital to keep in mind that the only thing you have to prove is your ability to use English, not that you have made the best choice of the topic.

You are on a committee that must recommend a student for a University Scholarship for biological science studies. There are four final candidates. Look at the notes describing each potential scholarship recipients and after discussing their advantages and drawbacks propose the best candidate to the head of the selection committee.

Candidate A

Katerina Papa
- Comes from a single-parent family – economic in need
- High grades in Biology and Chemistry
- President of science club
- Involved in charity work
- Popular with his classmates
- Doesn't want to leave his hometown

Poly Kara
- Highest grades in the school
- Interested in political issues, especially feminism
- Not afraid to explore new things
- Honest and reliable
- Very athletic – plays in three teams
- Hasn't decided if she wants to study biology or physics

Candidate B

Steve Smith
- Very popular student – class president
- Has always wanted to be a scientist
- Parents are both biologists
- Good at following direction and adhere to rules
- Dominates discussions and conversations
- Average grades, but he doesn't study hard

Ronald Kopa
- Deeply interested in maths and physics
- Enjoys reading and doing research papers
- Second highest grade in the school
- Very intelligent and hard-working
- Comes from a large family – parents can't afford university education
- Not very sociable or self-confident
- He has only few friends

Stage I: Introduction/Breaking the ice - Small Talk (3-5 minutes)

These questions are hard to be foreseen. Use the methodology presented in the previous chapters and summarized in table 17. Furthermore, this Stage has been already covered in section A.

Stage II: Presenting, Summarizing and Recommending (5-7 minutes)

(At this stage, the topic of the speaking task will be introduced and instructions will be provided.)

First Examiner*: O.K. Now let's move on to Stage II and let me introduce you to the topic under discussion.*

You have been asked by the head of the selection committee to serve on to select the most suitable student for a University Scholarship for biological science studies. Here is some information about the four final candidates. Each of you will be given a sheet with brief notes about only two of them.

You will have 2-3 minutes to look at the information you are given. When you're ready, one of you will describe your two candidates, to your partner using your own words and provide as much detail as you can, based on the information you have. At the same time, your partner will be listening and then in the end will be asked to give his(/her) opinion about which of the two he/she thinks deserves to be selected as next year's scholarship recipient. You do not need to memorize anything, as you may look at your sheet whenever you wish, but you are not allowed to look at your partner's sheet. Furthermore, If you wish, you may take notes, but there is no need since you are free at any time to ask your partner to repeat or clarify any of the information he(/she) is presenting.

Then you will switch roles. In the end, you will have to narrow your choices down to one of the four and present it to the head of the selection committee.

If you have any questions about the instructions, please feel free to ask. (The first Examiner hands out information sheets.)

First Examiner: *Now I'd like you to take a minute or two to decide silently which of your own two students you think is better to be awarded the scholarship. Remember that either candidate is good, but you need to select only one. When you are ready, we will move on to Stage III.*

[The first Examiner is silent while candidates think]

First Examiner*: Now for Stage III. I'd like you to work with your partner and to take turns reporting to each other which student you chose.*

First Examiner*: Now, at this stage, you will have to cooperate and narrow your choices down to one out of the two.*

You need to contrast and compare your choices until you agree on the option that you think is the best. Your goal is to choose the best option. Remember that either option is good, but you need to select only one. You also need to give the reasons for your final decision and explain why they are important. Remember that you are not allowed to look at each other's sheet.

Stage IV: Presenting and Convincing (5-7 minutes)

(At this stage Candidates formally present their final decision to the second Examiner. They are now allowed to share the sheet containing the information concerning their final choice while collaborating with each other IN ENGLISH to prepare a convincing presentation)

First Examiner: *O.K. this is fine. In the final stage, you are asked to formally present your decision to the head of the selection committee and persuade him/her that the choice you've made is the best.*

I'll give you 2-3 minutes to plan your presentation and which reasons you will each present. You must convince him/her that your choice is the best. You may at this point read each other's sheet. You must each present two different reasons and explain why they are important justifying your choice. After your presentation, the head of the committee will ask you some questions.

Second Examiner: *Hello. My name is... and I am ready to listen to your choice.*

[When they finish their presentation the second Examiner begins last stage.]
Second Examiner: *Now I'd like to ask you a few questions to make sure I understand your decision.*
Try to figure out what his/her question may be, according your final choice and its features. Formulate his/her potential question

> *Are you really sure we should select...? I understand your reasoning, but what do you have to say about the fact that... ? Isn't this a disadvantage?*

———————————————————————————
———————————————————————————
———————————————————————————
———————————————————————————
———————————————————————————
———————————————————————————
———————————————————————————

Give your answer

———————————————————————————
———————————————————————————
———————————————————————————
———————————————————————————
———————————————————————————
———————————————————————————
———————————————————————————
———————————————————————————
———————————————————————————
———————————————————————————
———————————————————————————
———————————————————————————
———————————————————————————
———————————————————————————
———————————————————————————
———————————————————————————

Second Examiner: *This may be true. What is also true though is that at least two of the other candidates are certainly worth choosing if we take a closer look at their qualifications. For example...*

Now, Try to figure out what his/her second question may be and formulate it.

Give your answer

(The second Examiner closes the speaking test and thanks the candidates for their presentation)

Second Examiner: *Well, all right then. I'd like to thank you both for your input. We'll be sure to take your comments into account when we make our final decision. Thank you for your time and you are free to go.*

Respond using appropriate phrases from **Table 9**.

____

____

____

____

____

____

____

PART IV

SPEAKING PROMPTS

Possible topics (or more accurately tasks or role playing) that may be come up during the Speaking Test are presented in *Table 24*. A general list of information related to these tasks can be found in *Table 25*. Of course, they are in no way an exhaustive presentation of all possible instances. To practice, choose some of these pieces of information, that may describe a potential candidacy, either a person, or a trip, or something else, and try to rephrase them. Next, present them in a brief and cohesive paragraph, combining similar features and referring to the negative aspect as well, like in the case with the previously presented example. This list can help you get acquainted with the most frequent features that may appear in the ECPE Speaking Test so that you are not taken aback. At the end of this part you can find some additional speaking cards that you can use for practice.

Table 24. Typical Speaking Test's topics that may be encountered in the ECPE Speaking Test

General category	Prompt example
General introductory wording	Somebody (student council, the local school board, some friends of yours) has/have asked you to (to serve on a committee to) **or** You have been asked by a person (student council, the local school board, some friends of yours) (to serve on/to join a local/national/public/ company's committee) to **or** You are members/part of a (high school, hiring) committee/ on a committee to/(travel) agency/class representatives and have(/that has) been asked to/that must
Recommend *(hire, select, choose)* ***a person***	<ul><li>recommend the best candidate for school president</li><li>select one student who will receive the Student of the Year award</li><li>select the most suitable scholarship recipient</li><li>recommend a student for the "… University Scholarship for … (e.g. Legal/Natural) Studies"</li><li>hire a coach for the local sports centre</li><li>recommend the most suitable (Basketball) Coach for the Sports Centre/local High School</li><li>select a person to represent your country at the International Youth Parliament</li><li>choose the most suitable New Director of the...</li><li>recommend the "Employee of the Month" of...</li><li>recommend the most suitable new executive chef for a</li></ul>

Table 24. Typical Speaking Test's topics that may be encountered in the ECPE Speaking Test

General category	Prompt example
	five-star restaurant • recommend the most suitable new chef for a traditional restaurant • select the best scientist to be the subject of a documentary film aimed at...
Recommend (select, choose) **an agency**	• **select an advertising agency** for a campaign encouraging young people to... (e.g. eat healthy food/pursue more active life, etc.)
Recommend a project	• decide how to spend a sum of money that you collected so as to contribute to a worthy cause • decide how to spend (a) $50,000 (Grant)... e.g. on School Improvements/ for the improvement of a specific National Park • select the project that will receive funding • select the best science trip for your class • book an one-month holiday for a family • choose an Exhibition for a Small-Town Museum • decide which Fund-Raiser to hold it
Recommend (select, choose, present) **a place (location)**	• present possible locations for the next Olympic Games • select the best proposal for the location of a landfill • choose a location for a new university • select a city site to be restored • select a location for a new manufacturing plant • present possible houses for rent
Recommend a learning program/course	• choose a Spanish Abroad Program for your High School • select a Personal Development Course for its personnel • choose a Summer Course for your School's students
Recommend a gift/ a Pet	• buy a gift for your cousin • adopt a shelter dog for your kids
Recommend a College	• propose the most suitable Colleges
Ending wording	**You have to decide among four options.**

Recommend a person **Young people/Students/ Older People/for work/grant/promotion**

Achievements

- He is an inventor. Developed
  - a car that can fly
  - environmentally friendly car
  - treatment for AIDS
  - very advanced (/superior) lie-detector
  - His previous discoveries have saved thousands of lives
- Former state champion
- High scorer on high school basketball team
- His team won state championship his last year
- Black belt in judo
- His students have a 100% success rate
- All her private students got into good universities
- Did a good job of training new staff (/personnel)
- Increased department sales introducing very interesting new products
- Increased the productivity in his department up to 20%
- Steady increase in productivity over the years
- Captain of school debating team
- Class president
- Founded and runs
  - school chess club
  - school environmental group
  - the institute Inventors for the Environment

Activities

- Active member of debating society
- Cheerleader
- Member of
  - school sports teams
  - local political organization
  - various volunteer groups
- Gives
  - free music lessons at the junior high school
  - talks to schools and colleges
- Helps
  - at a centre for children with learning difficulties
  - at organizing school music concerts
  - at running a soccer club for disadvantaged kids

	• Actively involved
	  o in environmental projects
	  o in charity (/philanthropy/) work
	  o in school band
	  o in theatre group
	• Organized
	  o boys' basketball league
	  o school recycling program
	  o science workshops for disadvantaged (/underprivileged/ deprived) kids
	
	• Volunteer coach
	  o basketball team of teenage girls
	  o for overweight children
	• Volunteer work
	  o after earthquake in...
	  o in the aftermath (/what follows) of Hurricane...
	• Has spent time abroad
	• Has travelled widely overseas
	• Writes
	  o about politics,..., ... for school magazine
	  o poetry in Spanish
	• Plays
	  o piano
	  o the drums in school band
	• Is leader of a youth group

Age	• Female, 29 years old • Male, Age 25
Appearance	• Has a sweet look which makes her look young and suitable • Looks young enough to be a baby-sitter

Ambitions/ Interests	• Has always wanted to be a... (e.g. lawyer)
	• Sets very high standards
	• Wants full-time position – change of career
	• Deeply interested in
	  o Law/politics/ political issues
	  o History/physics/science

Availability	• Only available evenings and weekends and unavailable afternoons • So busy that she is hard to find

Awards	• Excellent actress though no Academy Award
	• Winner
	   o of an Academy Award (/prize)
	   o of an Young Inventor competition/award
	   o of a national science contest (/competition)
	   o of an youth triathlon
	   o of the "Athlete of the Year" award
	   o of the "Best Employee" award at the...
	   o of the National song-writing competition
	   o of the 1995 Sports Teacher of the Year award

Creativity	• Has many ideas for future gadgets (/device) • Has set up his/her own business
Current job/ Duration	• Assistant athletic coordinator for... (5 years) • Elementary school gym teacher at a private school (2 years) • Teaches coaching clinics for... (5 years) • Hired 6 months ago • Case worker (/somebody assigned to provide social services), Child Welfare Department (/services aiming at protecting children) (3 years) • Director, ... (where: e.g. Organization of ...) (2 years) • Management position, ... (where: e.g. World Bank) (10 years) • Works as a tour guide during school vacations • Works part-time (in parents' store) to pay for... • Plays in a basketball league
Education/ Study/Training	• Attended college with ... as major; full scholarship • Degree in... • Majored in... with honors at age... • Master's degree in... from School of... from major university • Wrote master's thesis on... • Finished her Master's degree with honors • Is a recent graduate • Recent graduate of a top... (e.g. engineering) school

	• No formal... training (/coaching process/ practice) • Certified/Qualified paramedic (/emergency medic)/physical therapist/nutritionist (/expert in healthy eating) • Takes... classes in the evening • Two years certified coach for... • Was apprentice (/trainee/learner) under one of the greatest... • Fully qualified... • Fluent in English and French • Good level of spoken English • Speaks English, German, French, Danish • English – average • Does not speak English well • Studying Japanese • Written English weak • Mastered English first year in the USA • Lived in the USA until age nine
Family Status	• Family with 3 children • Has 4 kids of his own • Has no children so loves her students • Parents are both... (profession) • Comes from a large family – parents can't afford... • Comes from a single – parent family – in economic need • Middle-class family
Negative traits/Points	• Had argument in public with co-worker/ head office manager • Co-workers resent (/feel aggrieved at) him as he often works late to get the job done • Known to be temperamental (/loses temper easily/moody) and difficult to work with • Not reliable. Never punctual (/exact/accurate), often late for work • Impatient (/anxious/eager) with customers • Not so good at working under pressure • Long-lasting (/enduring/durable) leave-of-absence (/time off /permission for time off) last year to recover (/regain health) from... • A dyslexic student with learning difficulties • Unreliable (/untrustworthy/ irresponsible/not trustable) and changes plans last minute

- Hasn't decided if she wants to study... or...
- Brightly dyed hair and face piercings
- Not very creative (/productive/original/innovative)
- Can be boring (/uninteresting/of no interest)
- Doesn't share ideas with other people (/introvert/secretive)
- Can be too bossy (/controlling) and dominate (/have control over/ be predominant/prevail) discussions and conversations
- Wants total control over... (–ing) and...
- Overconfident (/too self-assured) and arrogant
- Not very sociable (/friendly/outgoing) or self-confident (/assured about oneself)
- A bit distant and reserved (/cautious/guarded/offish/uncommunicative/ gingerly/restrained/quiet/introverted)
- Doesn't have many friends (/anti-social/ unfriendly/ shy)
- Not a team player
- Might be a little too old and may not suit a... role
- Too feminine (/womanish) and not girlish enough
- Plans to leave the company next year
- Retiring in three months
- Very shy with students
- Assigns (/delegate/commend to/charge with/allocate) a lot of homework
- Doesn't like weak students
- Has lost her students' papers (/academic article/schoolwork/graded essay)
- Not very good at delegating tasks
- Parents at current school complain that he is too strict with young students
- Isn't good at decision making without others' advice
- Lacks people skills (/aptitude /aptitude/ability)
- Never traveled abroad before
- Doesn't want to leave his hometown
- Cannot travel for longer than... at a time
- Very expensive (/costing a large amount). Most expensive of the other candidates (/nominee/applicant)

Table 25. A general list of information related to possible topics that may come up during the Speaking Test.

Personality traits	• Confident (/feeling certain) when speaking in public • Not afraid to speak her mind • Adept at... (doing something) (/expert/skilled) • Dedicated to (/devoted to/committed to) any commitment (/promise/promise/ engagement) she makes • Excellent organization skills/Well-organized and focused • Very creative (/original/innovative/ productive) lesson plans • Brilliant (/extremely smart) and personable (/pleasant) • Compassionate (/sympathetic/kind) • Disciplined • Dynamic (/energetic/active) • Entertaining (/amusing/humorous/recreative/interesting/recreational) • Enthusiastic (/keen/hopeful/eager/animated) • Extremely intelligent (/intellectual/ knowing/ smart/clever/ingenious/ brainy/knowledgeable/comprehensive/apprehensive) • Generous with... adj (/giving/not petty/bountiful/free-handed/munificent) • Gets along well with co-workers (/support, agree with) • Hard-working (/diligent/industrious) • Highly motivated (/enthusiastic/keen/provoked/ induced) • Humorous (/great sense of humor/ funny/entertaining/amusing) • Outgoing (/extroverted/extrovert/extravert) • Passionate about... (/easily aroused/somebody who cares/believes strongly/ impassioned) • Popular (/well liked/accessible/frequently encountered) • Quiet (/calm/peaceful/gentle/reserved/quiescent/tranquil/serene, still/ meek/mild) • Serious (/thoughtful/ important) • Strict manner (/enforcing rules/ exact/precise) but efficient (/effective/ profitable/productive/capable/able/competent/sufficient/skilful) • Studious (/diligent/fond of learning/bookish/careful, painstaking/attentive) • Very athletic - plays in three teams • Dependable (/reliable/credible/trustworthy/trustable/trusty) • Friendly (/warm/sympathetic/kind/amicable) • Good looking (/attractive/ beautiful/handsome/shapely)

- Honest (/sincere/ upright/ truthful/ honest/fair/decent/honorable/ upstanding /straightforward/irreproachable/unimpeachable)
- Wide ranging responsibilities
- Excellent relationship with rest of staff
- Excellent work ethic and dedication
- Good public relations skills
- Good working relationships
- Good rapport (/good relationship) with colleagues
- Willing to learn
- Computer genius and science whiz (/wizard/person skilled at something)
- Loves her job (e.g. teaching)
- Works her students to the ground
- Does more than what the job description requires
- Works quickly and seldom makes errors
- Works well with others

Popularity

- Very popular (/well liked/accessible/frequently encountered)
    - with his classmates/ with his peers/among peers/with both students and teachers
    - fans love her/him
    - has loyal (/allegiance/loyalty) following among customers
    - as appeared frequently on television
- Voted (/selected/proclaimed/named/appointed)
    - smartest student by classmates
    - class president
    - one of greatest living scientists
- Colleagues admire (/respect/be impressed by/appreciate/estimate/assess/ value/evaluate/admire) him/her for his/her work
- Famous (/well-known) for his/her creative flair (/style/ability)
- Good reputation (/good repute/ high or favorable regard/fame/rumor) with colleagues/employers/students/parents
- Held in high regard (/esteem/great esteem/respect/consideration/name) by teachers

Skills	• Good at (/skilled/talented)
	  o explaining complex ideas in simple language
	  o persuasion and winning arguments
	• Good attention to detail
	• Good/Strong presentation skills
	• Keeps neat, accurate records
	• Knows how to
	  o get an idea across
	  o keep customers happy
	• Projects done on time
	• Multiple projects done on time (/multitasking)
	• Manages different projects at the same time
	• Encourages quality work
	• Emphasis on continuous improvement
	• Effective budget analysis and review
	• Enjoys being part of a team
	• Enjoys reading and doing research papers
	• Experienced public speaker

Study/Work track-records	• Honor student (/academic high achiever) • Straight-A student • Highest grades (/marks) in the school/in class • Second highest grade in school • Consistently high grades in... and... • High grades in all subjects • High grades in... and... • Grades just above average • Average grades, doesn't study much – could do better if she studied harder • Poor grades in academic subjects • Little involvement in class projects • Skips (/fail/miss out/omit/miss/leave out) classes frequently • No extracurricular activities
Traits related to position	• Recommended (/propose/suggest/offer/proffer/nominate) by head... • Willing (/ready/eager/complaisant/voluntary/compliant/keen to/agree freely to) to do... work • Very good at training new staff members • Created a better system for...

- Has played such a role
- Participated (/take part) in this activity two years ago
- Came up with (/appear/show up) now-popular idea of...
- Used to working long hours
- No absences or late arrivals

Work Experience

- 10 years experience at/in... (e.g. at the company)/as...
- Worked as... for 5/25 years
- Worked 20 years in...
- Worked 1 year as..., but has mastered job
- Skilled (/experienced/adept/practiced/skillful)... with 10 years' experience... with young children
- Specializes in the latest... (e.g. teaching/cooking) trends
- Has held 6 different... positions in last 10 years
- No practical experience as...
- President of debating club
- President of school athletic society
- Editor of school magazine
- Editor of the yearbook
- Knowledgeable (/knows a lot) in all areas of...
- Used to teach at a cookery college

Recommend a place
for a trip/business event/grant/rent/renovation

Accessibility

- Half a block from... very convenient to buses & trains
- Quite far from trains and buses
- Accessible (/reachable/easy to obtain/approachable/obtainable) by road
- Highways adjacent to (/beside) the city/run through the city
- One wide roads exists, minor road's use is restricted
- No access by road at all
- Two-hour bus ride each way
- Can fly direct
- Large international airport
- Small local airport
- Local airport is regional only/for domestic (/not foreign) flights
- Nine miles from... International Airport
- Limited transportation links, three hours to the nearest airport

Table 25. A general list of information related to possible topics that may come up during the Speaking Test.

	• Nearest highway/international airport around 150 miles away • Can go by ship • Good sea, rail and air transport links
Accommodation	• Accommodation (/lodging) in various parts of town • Student housing (/accommodation/sheltering) within university complex • Live in dormitory with other students • Dormitory close to many attractions (museums, galleries, shopping) • Students share a room with three or four fellow students • Live in on apartment in the centre of the city with 4 other students from your country • Live in homes of Spanish-speaking families • Ample accommodation facilities – leading tourist destination • All accommodation within walking distance of the... • On-site residence in a pleasant area of the city • Three 3-4 star hotels within walking distance from the... • Perfect apartment for anyone who loves... • Overnight accommodation/Staying in youth hostel • Very small rooms • Camping in mountains/in nature preserve • Sleep in log cabins • Students bring their own tents
Condition	• Relatively intact (/untouched/untouchable/unscathed/intangible/inviolate/unspoiled) cultural site • Beautiful historical (/historic) sites • Buildings with many representations, symbolism and ultra-modern design • Building to be demolished (/destroy/tear down/pull down) if not restored (/redintegrate/rehabilitate)
Cost	• $15 per student • $60.00 per week/month/year to maintain... • $2,000 to transport, install and insure • $2,000 for a 3-month subscription • Minimal course fees (/payment for service/admission, etc.) are only $100 per year

- Tickets: $25, $50 and $75
- Estimated expenses (/charge/outgoings/costs) $3,500
- Expenses (rental of cents, tables, seating, etc) about/approx. $3,000/1% of money raised
- Cheaper than other...
- Cheapest agency on the market
- Very reasonable (/logical/rational/sensible/satisfactory/fair/affordable) (room,...) prices
- Very Low Rent – Price: $800 Per Month
- Will be very economical (/not wasteful/using minimal resources)
- Not too expensive
- Inexpensive for visitors and participants
- Charge reasonable fees
- A bit expensive city
- A bit expensive for a three-week course
- Expensive conference room/accommodation rates/hobby/plane fare
- Rather expensive/high rental and accommodation fees
- Will be very expensive for athletes and fans
- Very expensive
- Accommodations/Real estate extremely expensive
- Government funding (/financing/financial support) available (/obtainable/ disposable/dispensable/expendable)
- Partly government subsidized (/fund)
- Costs paid for by grant from...
- Could get good local bands to play for free
- Grants available for sanctuary (/sacred place/ place of refuge/quiet place for somebody/asylum)
- Some private (/not public/personal/confidential) donations available for...
- Local businesses to donate (/give/contribute/offer/render/tender/ utter/grant/present) items to be auctioned (eg, furniture, artwork, kitchen appliances)
- Local businesses to donate...
- Volunteers to do live demonstrations (/show/expression/ display/show off/showing/manifestation) and work at...
- All arts on loan (/led/lending) (free of charge) from private collectors and local artists

	• Room discount for conference participants
	• School-sponsored groups admitted free of charge
	• Free admission for kids 12 and under
	• Free aquarium tickets
	• Discounted tickets to...
	• Special half-price offer to school groups
	• Walkers pay fee ($25) and get pledges (/promise) from others
	• Course fees must be paid in full at the point of enrolment
	• Can use school sports field at no cost
	• Admission includes viewing of award-winning film "... "
	• Catalogue/posters on sale at museum gift shop
Facilities (/amenities)	• Fully furnished luxurious 3 bedroom/2 bathroom apartment
	• Full kitchen, high ceilings, fireplace, hardwood floors, tile bath, large closets
	• Beautiful new stainless steel appliances in the entire kitchen
	• Luxurious rooms, state-of the-art design/equipment/fitness facility available
	• Gas, fireplace, hardwood floors throughout the apartment
	• Bright and airy apartment
	• Single Family Home
	• Basic facilities only - students must cook for themselves
	• 320-seat Auditorium/Conference room
	• Auditorium/Conference room capacity – 200/350/400/500 people/ up to 60 people
	• Audio/visual equipment, free high speed wireless internet access/connection
	• Conference rooms equipped to the highest standards
	• Technical support available
	• Conference/Video conference facilities available
	• Presentation's equipment is available
	• Outside Smoking OK
	• Dogs/Pets allowed
	• Luxury building with pools, spa, fitness center/club, swimming pool, bowling alley (narrow street/passage), children's play area
	• Excellent stadiums and sports facilities
	• International stadium for local team
	• Olympic stadium
	• Jogging track (/route/path)

- Tennis courts
- Bicycles available for rent
- Close campsite near waterfall
- Free covered car parking up to 70 cars
- Extra underground parking
- Huge parking lot/space
- Beautiful buildings
- Include cinema complex
- Major port with warehouse/cargo facilities
- Excellent leisure facilities for students
- An extensive activities program
- Restaurants, art galleries, shops, open-air market a short bus ride from most host-family homes

Food/Drinks

- On-site cafeteria
- On-site dining
- On-site restaurant
- On-campus cafeteria and restaurants nearby
- Provide shops and supermarket
- Excellent food, variety of dishes

Location

- Centrally located/Center of town and all facilities within walking distance
- Convenient location/Conveniently situated
    - equal distance from... and...
    - 3 miles from train station
    - close to highways
    - just 30 minutes from city center
- Situated/Located
    - at city's doorstep
    - in a western suburb (/outskirts)
    - outside town center
    - on the outskirts of the city
    - within easy reach of...
    - within walking distance
    - in an historical city
    - in a big city with many cultural attractions (/allurement/charm/joy/ spectacle/sight/show)
    - in a small rural town
    - in a depressed area (/poor region) of high unemployment

Table 25. A general list of information related to possible topics that may come up during the Speaking Test.

	o in a high crime area (might be vandalisms)
	o in a run-down neighborhood in need of renewal (/subscription/lease/ contract)
	o 30 miles from...
	o 12-hour drive from home

- Be housed in renovated 18th-century buildings
- Museums and other attractions within easy walking distance of most apartments
- Prestigious (/respected/having status) historic college on edge of a big city with lots of culture; 1 hour from home
- Famous landmarks
- Friendly (/warm/sympathetic/kind) to tourists
- Lovely (/nice/beautiful/handsome/fine) architecture
- Unique city – historical
- Unspoiled (/intact/untouched/untouchable/unscathed/intangible/inviolate) natural beauty
- Very colorful in spring
- Well-marked hiking trails

Negative traits

- Extra services (e.g. cleaning and laptops) can be provided for an additional fee
- Not very close to trains or supermarkets
- Facilities not open to local residents
- No Pets Allowed
- Non-Smoking
- No room discount for conference participants at nearby hotels
- Not enough accommodation facilities
- Old building
- Seems like it was abandoned overnight
- Needs major repairs
- Presenters need to bring their own laptop

People

- Cosmopolitan (/well travelled/multicultural) population
- Hospitable (/generous to guests) people
- 70% of population college graduates
- Large unskilled (/menial/not expert/inexperienced) labor force (/workers) available

Popularity/ Importance	<ul><li>Among the world's greatest monuments</li><li>Considered a World Heritage Site</li><li>Economically very strong</li><li>Home to two universities and a technical college</li><li>International reputation as leader in technological development</li><li>Popular (/well liked/accessible/frequently encountered) for all water sports</li><li>Voted (/selected/proclaimed/named/appointed) one of the Most Livable Cities</li></ul>
Population/ Size	<ul><li>Approximately (/nearly/close to) 90,000 people (/inhabitants/resident/ dweller/citizen/habitant)</li><li>Large, coastal town</li><li>Small, historic town</li></ul>
Remarkable characteristics	<ul><li>Trade zone with low costs for businesses</li><li>Icon of the... civilization</li><li>Improve image of town</li></ul>
Security/crime	<ul><li>Burglary (/break-in/stealing from home) rate is twice national average</li><li>Near neighborhood with high crime rate</li><li>High levels of crime</li><li>High local unemployment rate</li><li>Has promised tight security</li></ul>Spectators make noise and cause violence
Means of Transport	<ul><li>Poor/Excellent/Convenient public transportation (/public transport/public transit/mass transit) system</li><li>Modern transportation facilities</li><li>Traffic problems in and around the city</li></ul>
Weather/ Environment/ Temperature	<ul><li>Can get extremely hot in summer</li><li>High pollution levels, especially in summer</li><li>Quiet, rural atmosphere</li><li>Cooler weather</li><li>Very humid</li><li>16°C/23°C</li></ul>

	Recommend a class trip
Cost	(see Recommend a place)
Weather/ Environment/ Temperature	(see Recommend a place)
Time needed to get there	• A 4 hours by train • A 2 hour flight • A 4 hour flight and an 1-hour bus ride • 2½ hour drive/bus ride each way • One day and one night
Duration	• One day trip • Two days and one night • One day and one night
Food/Drinks	(see Recommend a place)
Accessibility	(see Recommend a place)
Location	(see Recommend a place)
Activities	• Visit animal sanctuary (/place of refuge) • Whale-watching tour • Bus trip to zoo • Field trip to a forest • Trip to alligator park • Stop at waterfall on way • Study native (/indigenous/ aboriginal) plant/animal species • Beach campfire on last night • Guided tour of space center • View replica (/copying/duplication/reproduction) of International Space Station • Realistic simulation (/recreation/reenactment) of shuttle launch • Explore our solar system using virtual reality technology • Measure pollution levels

Table 25. A general list of information related to possible topics that may come up during the Speaking Test.

	<ul><li>Carry out (/perform/conduct) experiments</li><li>Visit lots of museums</li><li>Air and Space Museum</li><li>Famous wax museum</li><li>Statue of Liberty</li><li>White House tour</li><li>Walking tour of national monuments</li><li>Tour of historic village</li><li>Tours of art museums</li><li>Golf lessons provided</li><li>Scuba diving lessons available</li><li>Optional river rafting</li></ul>
Available facilities	(see Recommend a place)
Accommodation	(see Recommend a place)
Negative aspects	<ul><li>... (e.g. canoeing) may be risky (/dangerous/hazardous/perilous/unsafe) if river is rough</li><li>Not recommended for people with fear of enclosed spaces (/claustrophobic/ persons who hate small spaces)</li><li>Not so easy to understand their speech</li><li>Only for students with passports</li><li>Parents must drive</li><li>Students may suffer from altitude sickness (/illness at high altitude)</li><li>Access to caves requires some rock climbing</li></ul>
Benefits	<ul><li>Learn<ul><li>about cave ecosystems, stalactites, and stalagmites</li><li>about endangered river species</li><li>how a DNA profile is created</li><li>to recognize objects in the night sky</li><li>about future applications of genetic research</li></ul></li><li>Question and answer session with scientists</li></ul>

Table 25. A general list of information related to possible topics that may come up during the Speaking Test.

Recommend a project	
Accessibility of the site	(see Recommend a place)
Actions required/ Consequences	• Food donations from supermarkets, restaurants • Food drive for local homeless shelter • Food sources – fruit trees and bushes on site • Demolition (/deliberate destruction) of some homes necessary • Permission needed from town council • Regular clean-ups by volunteers • Relocate riverside picnic area to grassy area near main entrance • Some habitat loss and increased pollution inevitable (/certain to happen/unavoidable) • Women do all the housework • Need to sell food and provide entertainment • Vehicles/adult drivers needed for food pick-up • Would require closing lab to students for an entire year
Cost of participation/ Admission Fees	(see Recommend a place)
Costs of the event/ organization/ Expenses	(see Recommend a place)
Current situation to be improved	• Complaints that lab not being used effectively; would need renovation (/restoration/repair) again in 5 years' time • Current children's hospital 75 years old; equipment badly outdated (/not modern/old-fashioned/no longer valid/obsolete) • Gym classes recently reduced from 3 times a week to once a week • Several local families lost homes in recent fire • Shelter about to close for lack of food • Globally, over 1.3 million lung-cancer deaths per year • Globally, over 2 million AIDS deaths each year • Over 1,500 people eligible (/entitled) in and around city, many without health insurance

Table 25. A general list of information related to possible topics that may come up during the Speaking Test.

Difficult/ negative point	• Over 50 species on display in climate-controlled cases simulating natural habitat, need to be improved/replaced • Local citizens unwilling (/not willing to/reluctant) to participate • Public highly critical of proposed restrictions • School officials aware (/conscious of/informed/knowing) that library usage has declined with increase in home Internet use • Visitor numbers limited - only science majors may participate • Walk to take place rain or shine • Bikes may be stolen or vandalized
Duration	• (see Recommend a class trip)
Economical Benefits	• Could raise $15,000 in sales (600 × $15 per ticket) • Event expected to raise $30,000 (before expenses) • More trees mean lower carbon emissions • More visitors means more revenue (/income/profit) • Proceeds (/money raised) to help build playroom for sick children • Project self-sustaining: increased revenue pays for cost of future maintenance (/conservation/preservation/subsistence/upkeep/support/keep/sustenance/keeping/observance/backing) • Upgrades → higher camping fees → more revenue
Facilities	(see Recommend a place)
Goal	• Future revenue to buy and maintain "green" electric buses • Modernize 20 current work stations and add 10 new stations • Open new trails (/path/pathway/footpath/lane) to now-inaccessible areas • Planned housing development near forest to be canceled • Plant new trees/vegetation to prevent (/stop/block/impede/hinder) erosion • Purchase (/buy) LCD projector for modeling experiments • Purchase new gym equipment, balls, nets, etc • Purchase of state-of-the-art firefighting helicopters • Remove dam (/water barrier) to return river to natural course (/state)

- Renovate school gym (last done 25 years ago)
- Renovate science lab (last done 20 years ago)
- Repave (/cover with new paving) and widen two main roads leading to park
- Replace all 30 computers with faster models
- Restore area now spoiled (/vitiated/worn/spoilt) by crime and graffiti
- Rock concert to raise money for local hospital
- Set up habitat conservation project
- Update collection, especially in science and history
- Update computer lab (last done 5 years ago)

Key Action

- A 10-mile walk to raise money for cancer research
- 2½ hour bus ride
- Add 5 more computer stations (bringing total to 10)
- Add new weight room and climbing wall
- Add staff to keep lab open after school
- Add up to 20 walkways to improve access for disabled visitors
- Flea market to raise money for fire victims
- Build 5 new campsites in wilderness areas
- Build new seating for spectators
- Buy new software covering more subject areas
- Buy safety equipment (goggles, aprons (/cook's protective garment), gloves)
- Clean and repair all park trails
- Create more comfortable, attractive reading areas
- Dinner and a play to raise money to buy insulin for low-income diabetes patients
- Employment for beach patrol officers
- Environmental clean-up of local riverfront area
- Equip network with high-speed Internet connection
- Indoor concert to raise money for AIDS research
- Measure pollution levels and carry out experiments

Other Actions

- Access to caves requires some rock climbing
- Bilingual exhibit labels in English and ...
- Distribution of fire safety information
- Donation boxes for money and cans of food to be put in schools, shops, etc
- Exhibit labels focus on how global warming is affecting...

Table 25. A general list of information related to possible topics that may come up during the Speaking Test.

	• Exhibition on job opportunities in genetics
	• Finds outside jobs for the patients
	• Free lecture series with local historians and artists as guest speakers
	• History of chocolate through photo displays and live chocolate-making demonstrations
	• Install all new flooring; current floor unsafe
	• Install new sprinkler system and smoke alarms
	• Install trash and recycling bins on trails
	• Lecture: future applications of genetic research
	• Play performed by local amateur actors' group
	• Dinner provided by local restaurant
	• Put up new signs to mark trails clearly
	• Students and adults needed to volunteer for clean-up crews
	• Students and families bring old things to sell
	• Name bands to perform free of charge
	• Replace old card catalog with online catalog
	• Tasting stations for visitors to sample chocolate from around the world
Other Benefits	• Gives hope to many people
	• Gives the disabled a chance to do something

	• Helps
	    o pay for professionals
	    o people of all ages
	    o protect marine ecosystems
	    o the disabled to train
	    o them learn independence
	    o them to find a job
	    o women of all ages

	• Improve school library (last done 10 years ago)
	• Improved access for tour buses/other large vehicles
	• Learn to live without drugs (/medicine/medication/medicament/narcotic/ dope/opiate)
	• Literally saves one human being
	• Lowers levels of air pollution in cities
	• May bring glory (honor/fame/splendor/magnificence/praise) to the country
	• May save a life
	• Raises environmental awareness in the community

Table 25. A general list of information related to possible topics that may come up during the Speaking Test.

- Teaches them to stand on their feet
- Teaches these people a skill
- Encourage citizens (/civilian/inhabitant/resident/dweller/ habitant) to cycle or walk
- Will help protect forest ecosystems
- Will improve health of citizens
- Will improve wellbeing (/health/happiness/prosperity/welfare/ prosperousness/euphoria) of residents
- Will increase diversity (/variety/diversity/multiculturalism) of urban wildlife
- Will increase tourism to the area
- Will increase value of property (possessions/land/real estate/ownership/ proprietorship/domain)
- Will reduce carbon footprint of citizens
- Will reduce traffic congestion (/overcrowding)
- Will reduce trash in coastal waters
- Will save millions in damaged property

Recommend a learning program/course

Cost	(see Recommend a place)
To be about (/on the subject of)	<ul><li>Advanced lessons of English/German/French</li><li>Theory of photography and advanced techniques</li><li>Food Safety and Knife Skills</li><li>Learn how to create the character, a setting and a plot in a short story</li><li>Learn the most important cooking fundamentals</li><li>Sauce Making Fundamentals</li><li>Course covers many areas of current nutritional issues: Vitamins – Energy needs – Nutrition and food habits</li><li>Learn photography online from anywhere in the world</li></ul>
Involves	<ul><li>Attend all-day intensive Spanish classes at private language school (20 students per class)</li><li>Attend classes at local high school (2,000 students) from 9:00-15:00: all subjects taught in German</li><li>Attend math, French history and science classes at local school in morning (1,000 students)</li><li>Classes taught exclusively in Spanish</li></ul>

	• Direct feedback on your photos from world-acclaimed, professional photographers. • Football training sessions and supervised games with professional coaches • High quality Italian course in the heart of Venice
Included	• A lot of social activities that help students make friends during the course • All study materials • Detailed instructional study guide • Each student assigned a student mentor who speaks no English • Extra language classes and cultural events in the evenings • Free deep relaxation CD • Free in-depth textbook on Nutrition • Full Tutor (/private teacher) and Admin (/abbreviation of administration/ paperwork/administrative) support • German classes with native teachers, all of whom have years of experience in teaching German to foreign students • Get your photos critiqued every week • Highly-qualified, native teachers • Homework assignment, quizzes • Includes videos, texts, web links, chat, forum • Instructor support • Intensive language study in afternoon (10 students per class) • Native, French speaking teachers provide an interesting French course
Special Features	• Go far beyond any book or DVD • Join students from around the world • Learn at your pace • Ideal for a complete beginner with an interest in food and health • Lessons run at a range of levels, so the course is suitable for beginners and long-time German language students alike • Many students and teachers speak English • On completion of your course, you will receive a diploma • Personal attention given to each and every student • Unlimited access to filmed recipes • The classes are made up of a maximum of 15 young students • The course consists of 20 French lessons per week, with each lesson lasting 45 minutes

	• Exceptionally welcoming, supportive staff in the school
Accommodation	(see Recommend a place)
Location	(see Recommend a place)
Activities	• Extensive cultural program, offering many activities and trips around the area • Extensive range of organized activities and excursions • Weekend excursions outside of the city (beach, forest, plains) • Week-long excursion to... at the end of course
Place Features	• City population: over 3 million/over 75,000 • Course based in..., an exciting city, full of culture and history
Course duration	• 30 days • A 24-hour supervision
Other Facilities	(see Recommend a place)
Negative Points	• Experience or previous qualifications requirement for enrolment (/university, college: registration) on this course • No organized excursions
Recommend a College	
Total Students	• 3,000/14,000/30,000 undergraduate students
Students per Class	• Average class size • 15 (small seminars) • 25 (seminars + some lectures) • 55 (lectures and seminars) • 150 (mostly lectures)
Tuition Cost	• $12.000/34,000 a year
Ranged	• Ranked 15th/45th on list of top 50 small colleges • Ranked 9th/25th out of top 40 large universities
Scholarship	• $10,000/25,000 for the first year/each year • Offering a full tuition scholarship
Location	(see Recommend a place)

Table 25. A general list of information related to possible topics that may come up during the Speaking Test.

	Recommend a gift
Gift	<ul><li>Puppy</li><li>Tracksuit (/athlete's trouser suit)</li><li>MP3 player</li><li>Artist's kit</li><li>A Gold Ring</li><li>Expensive Watch</li><li>Pearl Necklace</li><li>Silver Bracelet</li></ul>
Positive Feature	<ul><li>Comfortable and warm</li><li>Convenient to carry</li><li>Creative hobby – can encourage talent</li><li>Cute and loveable</li><li>Every girl should have one</li><li>Good for social life – meet other dog owners</li><li>Artistic personality – appreciate it</li><li>Status symbol</li><li>Teaches independence and responsibility</li><li>Versatile (/of many uses)– can be worn at school or for play</li><li>Very fashionable/ modern – popular brand</li><li>Walking a dog improves fitness</li><li>Water-resistant fabric</li><li>More productive than computer games/TV</li><li>Paints, paper and instruction book for beginners</li><li>Provides entertainment</li></ul>
Negative Feature/ Point	<ul><li>Colorful – might not like it</li><li>May be too mature a gift</li><li>Not sure about parents' reaction</li><li>Quite expensive</li><li>Quite heavy</li><li>Very conservative</li><li>May too formal</li></ul>

What can be done with it	<ul><li>Can be worn all the time</li><li>Create artwork and sell it to friends/family</li><li>Get it engraved</li><li>Good companion</li><li>Share favorite songs with friends</li><li>She'll wear it every day</li><li>Will encourage him/her to do sports</li></ul>
Recommend a pet (dog)	
Pet's Age	<ul><li>18 months</li><li>3 years</li></ul>
Size/Gender	<ul><li>Large male (about 50 kg)</li><li>Medium sized female (about 20 kg)</li><li>Small female (about 10 kg)</li><li>Could reach 60-70 kg fully grown</li></ul>
House-training	<ul><li>Needs some obedience training</li><li>Star pupil at obedience school</li><li>Obedience school a must</li></ul>
Past Owner	<ul><li>Neglected by previous owner</li><li>Past owner: elderly woman now in nursing home</li><li>Used to live on the streets</li></ul>
Appearance/ Physical Features	<ul><li>Short black/dark-brown coat</li><li>Long, red coat</li><li>Thick, curly white coat</li><li>Shedding (/lose fur) a problem; needs frequent brushing</li><li>Professional grooming (/brushing) at a dog salon a must (2-3 times a year)</li><li>Slight limp from leg injury before rescued by shelter</li></ul>
Behavior	<ul><li>Mistrusting at first may snap unexpectedly</li><li>Fond of shoes</li><li>Sometimes aggressive with strangers</li><li>Friendly, very active</li><li>Quit, gentle giant</li><li>Nervous around strangers</li><li>Loving, but overly playful</li><li>Needs extra love and medical supervision (/oversight)</li></ul>

Table 25. A general list of information related to possible topics that may come up during the Speaking Test.

	Recommend an agency or a company
Experience	• Company set up four years ago • Only been in business for two years • In business for 10 years • Operating for over 20 years • Highly qualified, experienced team • Have done campaigns for major international brands • Done several health campaigns • Little experience with youth market • Never done a health-related campaign • Specialize in...
Cost	(see Recommend a place)
Company size	• Small, family-run company • Young, enthusiastic team
Achievements	• Won awards for previous campaigns • Previous campaign promoting sports was highly acclaimed (/praised, gained popularity) • Guarantees never to go over budget • Reputation for sticking to deadlines
Negative Point	• Ads tend to be quite conservative in design
Special Features	• Produces imaginative (/inventive/ ingenious/creative) computer and graphic animation • Involve clients in creative process
	Recommend an Hobby/Sport
Safety	• Can be dangerous (/risky/hazardous/perilous/unsafe) • Can hurt your back • Must be in good shape • No second chances if something goes wrong

Availability	• Different program every day • Only afternoon hours available for adults • Open 9 am to 9 pm
Facilities	(see Recommend a place)
Benefit	• Very good exercise • Can be lots of fun • Don't need equipment • Exciting to soar (/go up rapidly/go upwards/fly without propulsion) like a bird • Can be done almost anywhere in the country • Helps you get around with no expense • Many locations available • Builds up your endurance (/stamina) • Gets you into great shape • Meet many interesting people • Swimming is excellent exercise • Very vigorous (/energetic) exercise
Cost	(see Recommend a place)
Requirements	• Need to take lessons first • Need to travel to find appropriate location • Should have good partner • Always need a partner • Don't need a partner • Must buy/ Need to get equipment/a racket and balls/ good sport shoes • Must know how to use safety equipment (/machines/furnishings, tools) • Needs strong arms and legs
Popularity	• It's the new fashion (/fad/trend) • Many young people are interested
Miscellaneous	• Can attend as often as you like • Can go alone if one of you is busy

You are members of education committee of your company and have been asked to recommend a learning program for the company's personnel. This course would be more entertaining rather than educational. You have to decide among four options.

CANDIDATE A

Option 1: Learning French

- Advanced lessons of French

- $150.00 per month

- 3 months

- Course is hold in an exciting city near Paris, full of culture and history

- The course consists of 20 French lessons per week, with each lesson lasting 45 minutes

- Experience or previous qualifications requirement for enrolment on this course

Option 2: Photo World

- Theory of photography and advanced techniques

- $350.00

- 1 year

- Internet-based course without fixed time schedule

- Get your photos critiqued every week

- Week-long excursion to local Natural Conservation Park at the end of course (optional)

CANDIDATE B

Option 1: Novel writing

- Learn how to create the character, a setting and a plot in a short story

- $80.00 per week

- 30 days

- Course is based in distance learning

- Join students from around the world

- Included all study materials

Option 2: Cooking

- Sauce Making Fundamentals

- $60.00 per week

- 45 days

- High quality Italian course in the heart of Venice

- Classes taught exclusively in Italian

- Course covers also many areas of healthy eating habits

You are members of a selection committee of your high school and have been asked to decide on the location for a school trip in the spring. This location should provide not only educational opportunities but also entertaining facilities. You have to decide among four options.

CANDIDATE A

Option 1: Paris

- 3-hour flight / 4 days' duration
- 18°C
- live in dormitory with other students
- $450 per student
- free Disneyland tickets
- only for students with passports

Option 2: Cyprus

- 2-hour flight / 4 days' duration
- 31°C
- three 3-4 star hotels. Students share a room with three or four fellow students
- $350 per student
- trip to aqua-park
- beautiful historical sites

CANDIDATE B

Option 1: Mountain Borras

- 5-hour car drive/ 5 days' duration
- 10°C
- $150 per student
- sleep in log cabins
- relatively intact natural site
- tour of historic cities

Option 2: Athens

- 4 hours by train/ 3 days' duration
- 23°C
- $200 per student
- all accommodation within walking distance of the historical city's centre
- bus trip to zoo
- overcrowded this time

You are members of a committee of your company and have been asked to decide on the employee of the month. You have to decide among four options.

CANDIDATE A

Option 1: Donald Nice

- Hired 6 months ago

- Did a good job of training new staff

- Has many ideas for future gadgets

- Impatient with customers

- Very popular among peers

- Knows how to get an idea across

Option 2: Mickey Pope

- Worked 2 years in this position but has mastered job

- Increased department sales introducing very interesting new products

- Sets very high standards

- Confident when speaking in public

- Projects done on time

- Is a recent graduate

CANDIDATE B

Option 1: Margareta Xanou

- 10 years experience at the company

- Increased the productivity in his department up to 20%

- Deeply interested in her efficiency

- No formal training

- Recommended by the Head of the Department

- Had argument in public with co-worker/ head office manager

Option 2: Poly Xenou

- Worked 20 years in similar positions

- Steady increase in productivity over the years

- Winner of the "Best Employee" award at her previous job

- Colleagues admire her for her work

- Used to working long hours

- Known to be temperamental (loses temper easily) and difficult to work with

Tips

- Once the decision-making task begins maintain eye contact with your partner.
- Refer to your information sheet, but try not to rely on it.
- Summarize the points presented on the information sheet for each option in your own words and not just read from the list. Paraphrase them.
- When summarizing information: Try to group your points, where possible.
- One point is usually negative. Don't forget to mention it in your summary.
- Rephrase the points by expanding them into full sentences and linking them together into a coherent summary.
- Your answers must be complete and to the point.

- Speak clearly, confidently and naturally.
- Don't worry about minor occasional mistakes and don't panic if you stumble for the right word.
- Be an active participant; but know when to give up your turn.
- Discuss each option carefully and develop the discussion.
- Listen to what the other candidate says.
- Make notes of the pros and the cons of your partner's option while you listen to his/her summary so that you can recommend the best choice.
- Smile. Breathe. Relax